TENNIS:
A Practical Learning Guide

By
D. RAY COLLINS, Ed.D.
Professor and Chairperson
Department of Health, Physical Education and Recreation
St. Cloud State University
St. Cloud, Minnesota

PATRICK B. HODGES, Ph.D.
Professor and Chairperson
Department of Physical Education and Athletics
Sinclair Community College
Dayton, Ohio

and

BETTY H. HAVEN, P.E.D.
Assistant Professor
Department of Physical Education
Indiana University
Bloomington, Indiana

Tichenor Publishing
P.O. Box 669, Bloomington, Indiana 47402

In Memory of
Alvin and Elsie Lee Collins
D.R.C.

and

In Honor of
Ramona and John Gurich
P.B.H.

and

In Honor of
Dr. John M. Cooper
B.H.H.

This book was published in the United States of America by Tichenor Publishing, a division of T.I.S. Enterprises.

ISBN 0-89917-436-1

Preface

At the time of this writing, our society's rate of participation in recreational sports and activities is at an all-time high, particularly in those leisure pursuits that promote improvement in cardiorespiratory function. Tennis is one of the sports that develops endurance of the cardiorespiratory system and also demonstrates value for achieving weight control. Participation in tennis also provides psychological benefits. The sport has traditionally served as a satisfying emotional outlet for millions of Americans.

Tennis enthusiasts must play regularly to realize the optimum benefits from the sport. Those who play more often generally perform at a level nearer to their potential. To play at maximum proficiency is the major objective of most tennis players. We feel certain that your study and application of pertinent information in this book will greatly assist you in your progress toward that end. The text is designed as a learning resource for beginning and intermediate level players, but the more advanced player can also benefit from its contents, particularly the chapter on stroke mechanics.

One advantage this book affords over most instructional texts in tennis is the use of high-speed photography to help describe the mechanics that are necessary to correctly perform the various tennis strokes. The book also accomodates both students and instructors with useful skills tests. Students will find certain test items valuable for use in practice drills and for self-testing. Instructors can use the tests effectively for classifying students by ability level or for measuring student achievement.

We are indebted to Andy Greenlee and Mike Hegstrom for allowing us to film their playing form for stroke illustration purposes. Also a special thank you to Fine Light Studios of Bloomington, Indiana for photographing the subjects with the Canon High Speed F-1 Camera on loan from Canon U.S.A., Inc., Photographic Products Division, Elmhurst, Illinois.

Gratitude is expressed to Pat Krueger for her quality work in rendering the book's many illustrations. Appreciation is extended to Ray's wife, Phyllis, for her proficiency in typing the manuscript. A special thanks goes to the management of Fitzharris Athletic Supply Company of St. Cloud, Minnesota, for providing the assortment of tennis rackets pictorially displayed herein. We are also grateful to the instructional development unit of St. Cloud State University for designing and producing the equipment photos presented in Chapter I.

Contents

I

Getting to Know Tennis

Tennis is a popular sport in most of today's civilized world. The curriculum in educational institutions from elementary school through college commonly includes tennis instruction in the physical education program. Youth organizations and community recreation agencies routinely provide for their clients an opportunity to play tennis. Private tennis clubs serve as popular social organizations in many countries. The prominent place the sport holds in media sports coverage is another verification of its wide popularity. The scope of involvement in the sport ranges from the raw novice in informal play to the professional performer who competes for millions of dollars annually over much of the world. Either as participants or spectators, literally millions of people around the globe enjoy this invigorating sport.

In almost any American community, tennis courts are prominently visible in or adjacent to such areas as schools, parks, recreation centers and private homes. Many private and public clubs have indoor courts for year-round utilization, especially in the northern United States.

Tennis is a sport that can be learned or played at any age by both male and female participants. The enjoyable competition of the game provides social, physical and psychological benefits for players of all ability levels. It is a popular activity during all seasons of the year and requires only a modest financial investment (racket, balls and appropriate shoes), since outdoor courts are often available at no cost.

Tennis can also be a highly competitive game that involves both genuine athletic ability and vigorous physical stamina. There is no way to minimize the importance of the related skill development pertaining to such key variables as speed, agility, coordination, endurance, strength and mental toughness.

Like any other sport, tennis requires a great deal of practice and repetitive drill work in order for a player to measurably improve. Once the basic stroke mechanics are mastered, then the strategy phase of the game must be learned. No one should expect to play tennis for the first time and experience immediate success; it just does not happen. Tennis is an activity that definitely involves progressive skill development, but with proper instruction and much practice and patience, it can become an enjoyable social and competitive experience that helps the participant stay physically and mentally alert.

The impact of tennis upon the recreational, social and educational scene in America has been extraordinary. Over 200 instructional books have been published on the subject since Charles Tuckey's 1937 text appeared in print. Add all the autobiographies, memoirs and books of poems related to tennis, and the list becomes even more imposing. At least eight major tennis periodicals are currently published. More than a dozen national and international tennis organizations exist. The impressive listing of the above sources and organizations, along with major competition categories and player rating scales, are presented in the Bibliography and Appendix. Your review of these important sections of the text will enable you to better understand the vast scope of the tennis world.

HISTORY

Tracing the game of tennis from one particular origin is virtually impossible. A historical review indicates that a game resembling tennis was played as early as the time of the Greek and Roman Empires. The Chinese were hitting a ball back and forth with a crude racket more than 2,000 years ago, and around 500 B.C., the Egyptians and Persians played a type of racket game.

The historical picture becomes clearer when reviewing the thirteenth century. A French game similar to tennis, called *jeu de paume* ("sport of the hands"), was popular among the upper social classes, especially in Paris. Remnants of the playing courts have been found at Le Chateau du Louvre in Paris, dating back to the fourteenth century. The early game of *la paume* involved hitting a ball over a rope with the bare hands. The ball was made of wool or animal hair and was covered with sheepskin.

The popularity of the French game spread quickly throughout France, and the "commoners" were constructing simple courts in fields, barns and even monasteries. The monks found the game fascinating and were some of the better competitors. The game had spread to England and Holland by the end of the fourteenth century and was well on its way to becoming the popular activity it is today. Rackets were not introduced into the game until the end of the fifteenth century. The actual term "tennis" was probably derived from the French verb *tenez*, which means to take, hold or receive.

A few interesting pieces of historical information about French tennis feature King Louis X, who died in 1316 as a result of exposure to the elements while watching a match, and Charles IX of France, who was considered the first and youngest junior champion in 1552 at the age of two. During the last half of the sixteenth century, there were over 2,000 playing professionals in France, which created an immediate market for vice and gambling. The longest reigning acknowledged champion was Jacques Edmund Barre, a Frenchman, who held the number one ranking from 1829 to 1862. By the middle to late eighteenth century, the sport had virtually disappeared in France.

The modern game of tennis, as we know it today, was introduced in England by Major Walter Clopton Wingfield in 1873. According to one story, Major Wingfield, a former captain in the First Dragoon Guards and one of the honorable corps of Gentlemen-at-Arms at the court of Queen Victoria, was attending a rather elaborate house party at Nantclwyd Hall in Denbighshire. After awhile, the party was beginning to drag and the hostess asked for amusement ideas. Major Wingfield suggested a new game called "Sphairistike," which he described as a kind of outdoor tennis. He just happened to have with him the necessary rackets and balls, and fortunately, the guests found this new game to be very entertaining. Interestingly, the original Greek game of Sphairistike was played on a court that was shaped like an hourglass. It measured 60 feet long, 30 feet wide at the baselines, and 21 feet at the center, where a net was suspended. The net was seven feet high at the ends and sagged to a height of 4⅔ feet at the middle.

A second story involves Major T. H. Gem, who in 1858 had already marked a tennis court on a lawn in Edgbaston, a suburb of Birmingham, England. This game, referred to as "court tennis," "real tennis," "royal tennis," and even "lawn tennis," thrived in Edgbaston until 1870, when it was moved to Leamington and the lawns of the Manor House Hotel. A plaque is currently on the grounds that reads, "On this lawn in 1872, the first lawn tennis club in the world was founded."

Because of their early contributions, either Wingfield or Gem (or both) could be called the "Father of Lawn Tennis." Incidentally, the name "lawn tennis" is somewhat self-explanatory. In England, tennis was originally a game played outdoors on a lawn and nothing else. Today's game is played on a wide variety of surfaces, which probably accounts for the disappearance of the word "lawn" from accepted terminology relating to the game of tennis.

The All England Club, which is now known as Wimbledon, was founded in 1868 as a croquet club. In 1877, when the famous club was experiencing financial growing pains, a lawn tennis championship was held for the purpose of raising the required funds. The result was a financial success. Had there been no Wimbledon Lawn Tennis Championship, the first official lawn tennis tournament in the world, the sport of tennis would almost certainly have been different from what it has evolved into today.

The game quickly spread throughout England and then to the United States, and by 1880, nearly every major cricket and croquet club on the eastern coast of America had its own tennis courts. The biggest problem seemed to be a definite lack of standardization of the rules, so each club established its own. Finally, in 1881, a meeting of the leading East Coast clubs was held in hopes of standardizing the tennis rules. From this historic meeting came the founding of the United States Lawn Tennis Association

(USLTA), which later became the United States Tennis Association (USTA), the major governing body for tennis in the United States. The first United States Championship was held in Newport, Rhode Island, that same year.

Tennis has since had many true champions and well-known personalities such as Don Budge, Jack Kramer, Pancho Gonzales, Maureen Connolly, Althea Gibson, Ken Rosewall, Rod Laver, Arthur Ashe, plus many more. No sport has ever gained in popularity as rapidly as tennis did in the 1970s, due primarily to extended television coverage, "winner-take-all" matches and expanded tournament schedules accompanied by extensive financial support and large prize purses. The phenomenal growth has made tennis a worldwide and year-round sport. Names such as John Newcomb, Stan Smith, Ilie Nastase, Margaret Court Smith, Evonne Goolagong Cawley and Billie Jean King have brought tennis to the eye of the public. The decade of the 1980s belongs to such stars as Jimmy Connors, Bjorn Borg, John McEnroe, Chris Evert Lloyd, Martina Navratilova, Tracy Austin, Andrea Jaegar and Hana Mandlikova. And somewhere in either high school or college today is a little-known, developing player who very likely will emerge as the most accomplished player of the late 1980s and the early 1990s.

EQUIPMENT AND SUPPLIES

Racket

A very important prerequisite for successful tennis is a proper racket selection. Commonly asked questions concerning the choice of a racket are related to the type, shape, weight and size of the head and grip. Other more specific factors might include flexibility of the shaft, type of strings, amount of string tension and, of course, the cost.

The United States Tennis Association rules governing racket construction and design are very flexible. They simply indicate that the racket must consist of a frame and strings, and that the frame may be constructed of any material, in any weight, size or shape. The rules also state that the strings must be alternately interlaced or bonded and connected to the frame. No specific guidelines are given, which explains why there are dozens of racket designs to choose from on the market today.

There is no absolute right or wrong choice in the racket selection process with so many quality designs available. Whatever an individual feels comfortable with is satisfactory, providing that the guidelines for determining proper racket weight and grip size are followed. These guidelines are presented later in this section.

Composition. Prior to the last 12 to 15 years, the majority of tennis rackets were made of laminated hardwoods, and there was a basic standardization of dimensions. Since the mid-1960s, however, a racket composition of wood, fiberglass, graphite, steel, boron, aluminum, plastic, plus other hybrids of synthetic, wood or metal components has become

4

available. The current trend seems to be toward graphite or similar lightweight synthetic materials, which partially explains the reason for another trend, that of escalating costs.

The novice or beginning tennis player should start with a wooden racket, if for no other reason than the lesser cost. The wooden racket is still the most popular type used at all skill levels, not only for economic reasons but because it contains a stiffer shaft and is easier to control.

Head shapes. The shape of the racket head may be round, oblong, teardrop, rectangular, diamond-shaped or oversized. The oversized racket is becoming increasingly popular because it allows a player to return a greater number of balls that are hit off center. In other words, this feature reduces the number of errors in hitting judgment.

The oversized racket head is 100 square inches in size, as opposed to the traditional racket head, which measures 70 square inches. A midsized racket, with a head measuring 85 square inches, is also available today.

Regardless of the shape of your racket head, which again is an individual choice, the ball should consistently be hitting the "sweet spot," the area in the center of the racket face that provides for a more accurate, reliable and powerful return.

Fig. 1. Assortment of unstrung rackets, illustrating variety in composition and head design: (1) graphite-fiberglass/oblong; (2) laminated wood/round; (3) aluminum/oversized; (4) fiberglass-aluminum/round; (5) graphite-boron/teardrop; (6) graphite-boron/rectangular.

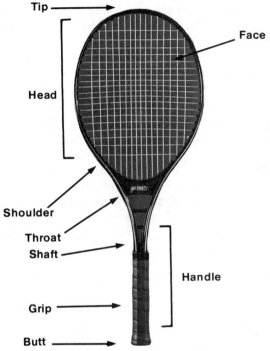

Fig. 2. Racket components.

Weight. The choice of racket weight is not so much an individual preference but instead should be directly related to body size and strength, plus the player's style of play. A racket that is too light or too heavy interferes with accuracy and control. For the player who favors an aggressive style of play, a lighter weight is preferable. A heavier racket is more suitable for the baseline player, who prefers to rally with ground strokes.

Racket weight categories are as follows:

Light: 11½—13 ounces (juniors and women)
Medium: 13½—14 ounces (older boys and men)
Heavy: 14½—15 ounces (big men or heavy hitters)

Along with weight, racket balance should be considered. The balance point of a racket is usually halfway between the butt and tip of a strung racket. On a 27 inch racket, the balance point is 13½ inches from the end of the racket. Again the choice relates to the individual style of play. A player who commonly hits powerful strokes from the baseline benefits from a slightly heavier racket head, while the aggressive spin player who goes for accuracy prefers a lighter head.

Grip. The size of the grip, or the circumference of the racket handle, is an important variable, since an incorrect grip size directly affects a player's proficiency. The size of the hand dictates the grip size. If the tip of your thumb touches the first joint of the middle finger while the racket is gripped at the base of the handle, a proper grip is assured.

Grip sizes range from 4¼ to 5 inches and vary in ⅛ inch intervals. The grip material is generally either rubber or leather, and its selection is basically a matter of individual preference.

Strings. Two basic types of strings are available. Gut, which comes from animal intestines, is a more resilient and expensive string, but it is also more sensitive to humidity and temperature and tends to fray more quickly. Gut must be replaced more often, at a greater expense, and it is not as popular as a result.

Nylon is a durable synthetic string that is less expensive but is close to gut in overall quality. For advanced players, gut does have an edge over nylon, but for the majority of tennis players, nylon is the recommended string. The different grades of available nylon string vary in quality and cost.

Strings come in 15–, 16– and 17-gauge thickness. The standard 15-gauge is recommended for most players. The 17-gauge is the thinnest and least durable but is most resilient; it is used primarily by tournament players.

String tension refers to how tight a racket is strung and is measured in pounds per square inch. This tension generally varies from 40 to 70 pounds, depending on the racket head type and flexibility, plus the style of the player. Gut, favored by the tournament players, is strung from 55 to 65 pounds, while nylon string tension ranges from 40 to 55 pounds. The recommended string tension for amateur players is around 45 to 55 pounds. As players improve, they tend to favor a higher string tension.

Many rackets come from the manufacturer already strung, so the choices have been made for you. Many do not, however, so a player looking for a good beginner's racket should ask for medium-grade, 15-gauge nylon strings with a tension of 50 pounds.

Cost. The cost of tennis rackets varies a great deal, all the way from $10 to $15 up to $200 or more. You should realize that an expensive racket is an unwise investment for a novice or beginner. A suggested price range for a beginner is $15 to $25; obviously the more skilled the player is, the more justifiable the financial investment becomes. The cost for stringing a racket ranges from $10 to $30, depending on the quality of the string.

Ball

Tennis balls are made by molding two cups of rubber and gluing them together. They are covered with wool felt and inflated with compressed air. The more durable "heavy-duty" balls are covered with more felt for longer play. Most balls are packed in a pressurized can (three per can), so they will retain their maximum bounce potential until used. Not all long-lasting balls are available in pressurized cans, as some are made from a special type of rubber that gives them resiliency. The pressureless balls last longer, but they feel "heavy" while playing, and they wear out racket strings at a faster rate. The United States Tennis Association recently banned non-pressurized or low-pressure balls from the International Tennis Championships, unless the use of such balls is agreed upon beforehand.

Ths USTA has very specific guidelines for what constitutes an acceptable ball. Each ball must have a uniform outer surface and should be either white or yellow. If there are seams, they must be stitchless. The ball diameter must be between 2½ and 2⅝ inches, and it must weigh between 2 and 2 1/16 ounces. When dropped from a height of 100 inches on concrete, the ball should bounce between 53 and 58 inches. Deformation guidelines are also specified but are not practical enough for the average tennis player to follow. Just remember that when in doubt, buy the balls that have the "USTA Approved" stamp on them.

In addition to white and yellow balls, there are orange and dual-colored balls available. The life span of a ball varies according to the court surface used, weather conditions and the player's style of play. Worn or "dead" balls may be used for drill work, but new balls or at least balls that are in good condition should be used in game play by players of all skill levels. This practice will help you guard against the development of bad habits that inconsistent bounces tend to promote.

Clothing and Accessories

In the early years of tennis, only white playing attire was acceptable. In fact, the dress code in tennis, both written and unwritten, was as strict as that of any sport in history.

Over the last decade, the fashion world has created an "open season" on tennis clothing. Dress guidelines have virtually disappeared with the creation of expensive matching tennis outfits that come in multicolor selections. Whatever you wear, it should be made of a "breathing" material such as cotton and should not restrict flexibility and movement. Coordinated outfits designed specifically for tennis are aesthetically appealing, but regular workout shorts, T-shirts, warm-ups or practically any outfit you choose to wear is suitable, providing it is safe and reasonable.

More important is the selection of appropriate tennis shoes. Because tennis is a fast-paced game that requires much quick movement, good tennis shoes are a must for preventing injury and allowing you to play at full potential. They do not have to be shoes designed specifically for tennis, but they should fit snugly, have a beveled or indented sole, and preferably should have a cushioned and arched insole.

Shoes are available within a wide cost range and are generally made of canvas. Canvas shoes are less expensive and "breathe" better but usually do not last as long. Whether the shoes are made of leather or canvas, look for a pair with a reinforced toe, since that is one of the first parts of the shoe to wear out.

The old adage, "A tennis shoe is only as good as the sock," might overemphasize the importance of socks but nevertheless contains a good deal of truth. Proper-fitting cotton socks are a necessity for preventing injuries and, particularly, painful blisters. Some tennis players prefer to wear two pairs of socks to provide additional cushion for the feet.

Some optional tennis accessories include wrist bands or head bands made of absorbent, elastic material that helps keep perspiration away from the hands and eyes. Tennis hats that keep down the glare of the sun are also popular. Sweaters, towels and even sunglasses are other common accessories. The main objective is to feel comfortable, dress safely, and have a good time.

COURT DESIGN

The USTA has very specific guidelines concerning court dimensions and permanent fixtures related to a tennis court. The court diagram shown in Figure 3 will enable you to become familiar with the court dimensions and markings.

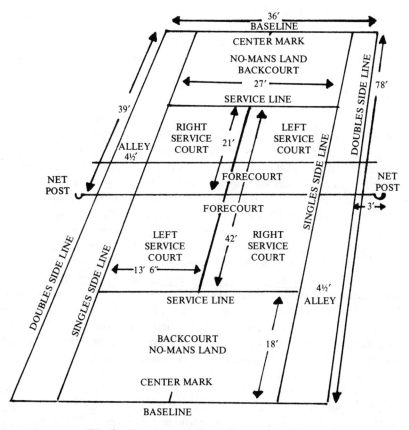

Fig. 3. Tennis court dimensions and markings.

A few other important regulations follow that pertain to the tennis net and court surface. The tennis net should be suspended from a cord or metal cable that has a maximum diameter of ⅓ inch, and the ends should be attached to the tops of the two net posts at a height of 3½ feet. The height of the net at the center should be 3 feet, and it should be held taut by a center strap. The net should completely fill the space between the two posts and touch the ground along its entire length.

Most tennis nets are made of a synthetic, flexible material such as nylon, or they are pretreated to withstand the adverse effects of moisture and severe temperature change. Metal nets are available and will outlast other types of nets, but they are not recommended for purchase. The metal nets have a tendency to bend or bow, which creates serious net height problems that are difficult to correct.

The other important aspect of a tennis court is the playing surface, which according to the USTA may be one of 100 or more surfaces, ranging from the original grass surface to asphalt, clay, concrete, cork, linoleum, plastic or wood. Most indoor and many outdoor courts are currently being built with a synthetic surface.

Some players play better on certain surfaces, depending on the stroke selection, strategy and style of play they favor. A beginning or intermediate player is not necessarily affected by the court surface, but to an avid tennis player who has developed a playing philosophy and strategy, it is a very important variable.

The three major categories of tennis court surfaces are hard, soft and synthetic. Hard courts made of concrete, asphalt or wood are the least common worldwide but are commonly found in the United States. This type of court requires very little maintenance and can withstand heavy and abusive traffic found at parks and educational institutions. It provides for a uniform, medium-high ball bounce and a "faster" style of play, which places more emphasis on the serve and return. A "big hitter" or a player with a strong serve tends to prefer the hard playing surface. Hard courts are often color-coded with a red playing surface and green border for increased visibility. The disadvantage of the hard surface is the ultimate wear and tear on the ball, shoes and the player's feet and legs.

Soft courts made of clay or a similar granular composition surface are the most common worldwide, especially in Europe. This type of court requires constant attention to keep in top playing condition. It must be swept, watered, rolled and lined daily, and it is adversely affected by weather conditions such as unusual temperatures and humidity. The soft courts are much easier on the balls, shoes, feet and legs, and a player is less likely to become tired or sore.

Clay courts create what is referred to as "slower" play, which means the ball bounces higher and slower off the rough surface. This obviously takes away from a "big hitter" or powerful server and places more emphasis on spin, accuracy and player quickness. The ball has a tendency to "sit up," which reduces the speed of the ball and increases the time an opponent has to reach the ball, thus creating longer rallies.

Synthetic courts made of composition materials are primarily found indoors and are becoming more popular due to the rapid rise of indoor facilities and winter professional circuits. The artificial "carpet" is very expensive to purchase and install, which is about the only major disadvantage. This type of court is a relatively soft, consistent surface that gives a uniform bounce somewhere in between clay and a hard surface. Although considered a "slow" surface, it is not as slow as most clay courts. The amount of slowness depends on the particular granular density of the surface being used. Synthetic courts are easy to maintain and can tolerate heavy traffic like a hard court. The fact that synthetic surfaces have many of the desirable characteristics of both the hard and soft surfaces partially explains their high cost.

The grass court is not considered to be one of the main court surfaces because it is the world's least common playing surface, especially in the United States. The word "lawn" has been dropped from most tennis organizational names simply because the game is seldom played on grass anymore. A few major tournaments, such as Wimbledon and the Australian Championships, still use the grass surface. Many of the top players do not like to play on grass because of its unpredictability. It is almost impossible to have a perfect grass surface, especially after play begins. Grass surfaces require more constant maintenance than clay courts, and bounces are often irregular and inconsistent.

OVERVIEW OF TENNIS

Basic Rules

The primary objective in tennis is to return the ball over the net into the opponent's court in such a way that he/she either is not able to return the shot or has difficulty hitting the ball back.

Tennis may be played by two (singles) or four (doubles) players, depending on personal preference. In singles, the server takes a position behind the baseline to the right of the center mark and proceeds to serve the ball over the net into the right service court, which is diagonally opposite the server's service court. If the first serve is unsuccessful (long, short or wide) and does not hit in the right service court, the server is then allowed a second serve.

Assuming either the first or second serve is good, the opponent or the receiver then attempts to hit the ball back over the net into any part of the singles court on the opponent's side. Play continues until a player is unsuccessful at hitting the ball over the net, or he/she hits it outside of the boundaries of the opponent's court or lets the ball bounce twice. A point is lost by the server when after two tries, he/she fails to place the ball inside the proper service court or on one of the lines enclosing the service court. A point is lost by the receiver if he/she does not return the ball directly over the net and into the opponent's court before the ball bounces twice. In order for a service return to be legal in tennis, the ball must clear the net and land in bounds after being hit, without first bouncing on the returner's side of the court. Of course, these restrictions apply to any return during a game.

As alluded to above, the service receiver must allow the ball to bounce once and only once before attempting the return. After the return of the serve, the ball may either be hit in the air before the first bounce (volley shot) or struck in between the first and second bounces.

When the server has made two unsuccessful attempts (double fault), he/she then moves to the left of the center mark and proceeds to play the second point of the game by attempting to serve the ball over the net into the left service court, which is diagonally opposite his/her service court. Should a served ball hit the top of the net and land in the proper service court, the serve is referred to as a "let" and is replayed without being counted as a fault. The right service court is also called the first service court, forehand service court or deuce court, while the left service court is called the second, backhand or ad court.

The server continues serving and alternating sides of the center mark for the duration of the game, or until one player wins at least four points with a minimum lead of two points (see scoring section, which follows). When the first game is completed, the players change ends or sides of the net, and the receiver in the first game becomes the server for the second game. At the completion of the second game, the player who served the first game again becomes the server, but the players do not change ends. The service role is exchanged after every game. Only after the completion of an odd-numbered game do the players switch ends. Play continues until one player wins the set, which means that he/she has won at least six games while holding at least a two-game lead. Competition continues until a match is completed, which happens when one of the players wins two sets. Sometimes in professional play, the first player to win three sets wins the match.

The rules for doubles tennis are identical to those for singles, with only the court dimensions being different. Each team plays the doubles court, which includes the alley on each side of the court. The baseline remains the same, as do the service court areas. The only potentially confusing aspect of doubles involves the service rotation. Assume players A and B are on the same side and they serve first. Therefore, they are initially the serving team. Players C and D are on the opposing side, and they are the receiving team for the first game. Player A serves a complete game, then players A and B switch ends with players C and D. Player C then serves a complete game, and player B does the same in the game that follows. Subsequent to player B's serve, which would be the third game, the teams switch ends and player D then serves the fourth game. For the fifth game, the rotation starts again with player A serving, followed by players C, B and D. This rotation continues until the set is completed. The rotation may be changed after the completion of a set but not during the set.

Only a basic overview of tennis rules has been presented here. For specific rules and regulations relating to all phases of tennis, read and study carefully the rules section of the Appendix.

Scoring

The scoring system for tennis is unique compared to that of other sports. The method of scoring is easy to comprehend, even though the terminology related to the points may seem odd at first. The first unusual thing to remember is that no points or zero points is referred to as "love," a term that comes from the French word *l'oeuf,* which means "egg" or shaped like a zero. (This has nothing to do with the romantic aspect of the English word "love," which obviously has a totally different meaning.) The first point of a game is labeled "15," with the second point being referred to as "30." The third point of the game is "40," which is not an increase of 15 as the first two points are. With a progression score of love, 15, 30 and 40, the next point scored (fourth point) ends the game, assuming the winning player is ahead by at least two points. The point that wins the game is called "game point."

Assume that the score is 40–30 or the server has scored three points and the opponent has scored two points with the losing player or receiver scoring the next point. The score is then called "deuce," which means the same as a tie score or in this case, 40–40. The term, "deuce," should only be used if each player has scored at least three points and the score is tied. Otherwise, it is 15–15 or 30–30, not deuce.

The server's score should always be stated first. For example, assume there is a deuce score and the server wins the next point. The score is then "ad in" or "advantage server," which means the server is ahead by one point. When the receiver wins the next point after deuce, the score is then "ad out" or "advantage receiver." If either player has the advantage and wins the next point, the game is over. In other words, it takes two consecutive points after a deuce score to win a game.

If the following scoring table seems logical based on the previous discussion, then you have mastered the scoring system in tennis.

Server Has Won		Receiver Has Won	Score Is	Total Points Scored
1	Point(s)	0	15–Love	1
1		1	15–15	2
1		2	15–30	3
1		3	15–40	4
2		3	30–40	5
3		3	Deuce (40–40)	6
4		3	Ad In	7
4		4	Deuce	8
4		5	Ad Out	9
5		5	Deuce	10
6		5	Ad In	11
7		5	Game	12

When the total number of points scored by both players is an even number, the serve should always be from the even or right side, and if the total is an odd number, the server serves from the odd or left side of the center mark. A set concludes when one player wins six games and is ahead by at least two games (e.g., 6–4). A set score could go from 5–5 to 6–5, which means that the set is not yet over. A 6–5 set score indicates that the server is ahead by only one game, yet in tennis a player or team must win by at least two games. A 7–5 score ends the set, but a 6–6 score indicates that the set must continue until one player wins by two games (e.g., 19–17), unless one of the acceptable tie-breaking procedures is in effect. A match consists of the best two of three sets (e.g., 6–3, 4–6, 6–4). Some professional matches consist of the best three of five sets.

The choice of tie-breakers is up to the players involved, except in tournament play, in which case the type of tie-breaking procedure must be predetermined. Marathon matches can be enjoyable for spectators, but they are exhausting for the players and are not suitable for tournament and television schedules. On the other hand, a tie-breaker or "sudden death" format can add a special excitement and suspense to the competition without requiring an excessive amount of time.

Tie-breaking regulations were deemed necessary by both the International Tennis Federation and United States Tennis Association, primarily for time control purposes as a favor to spectators and the television industry. In 1974, the ITF designated the 7-of-12-point tie-breaker as the official procedure. The USTA had previously used the 5-of-9-point tie-breaker, and it was not until 1980 that the USTA officially adopted the 12-point system. As a tennis player, you are likely to be involved with both tie-breaking procedures, so a brief explanation for both is presented here.

In the 5-of-9-point tie-breaker, the first player to win five points wins the set. When player A is due to serve the next game after a set score of 6–6, then player A proceeds to serve points one and two from the right and left courts, respectively. The opponent, or player B, then serves points three and four, also from the right and left courts. After the completion of the first four points, the players switch ends of the court, and player A serves points five and six if necessary. If a winner is not yet determined, player B serves points seven and eight. The score could potentially be 4–4 at this point, in which case player B serves point nine from the same end, with player A having the choice of receiving the serve from either the left or right service court. The final set score appears as 7–6, and both players remain on the same ends of the court for the first game of the next set. Player B serves the initial game.

In doubles, the format remains essentially the same. To illustrate, assume that players A and B are playing against players C and D. Player A serves the first two points from his/her normal serving end, followed by player D, who has been serving second on his/her team. He/she then serves points three and four. This change in the service rotation is necessary to keep the players serving from their regular ends. The teams change ends of the court after the fourth point, and player B serves points five and six, if necessary. Player C serves points seven, eight and nine. The receiving team (players A and B) has the choice of receiving the final point (ninth) in either the right or left service court. In the first game of the next set, either player C or D may serve first, with the teams remaining on the sides of the court they occupied during the last point of the tie-breaker.

In the 7-of-12-point tie-breaker, the first player to win seven points while holding a lead of two points or more wins the set. If player A is due to serve the next game after reaching a set score of 6–6, player A proceeds to serve the first point from the right court. Player B serves points two and three from the left and right courts, respectively. Player A then serves points four and five from the left and right courts. Player B serves the sixth point from the left court, and then the players switch ends of the court. Player B serves the seventh point from the right court, followed by player A's serving points eight and nine from the left and right court, if necessary. Player B serves the tenth and eleventh points (left and right) with player A serving point twelve from the left court. The point score could be 6–6, in which case the players again change ends and follow the same format until a winner is determined. The rotation starts over with point thirteen being played under the same format as the first one. The final set score is recorded as 7–6. The players change ends to start the next set, with player B serving the first game.

In doubles, the same format is followed, with each partner staying in the same service order but not necessarily serving from the same end as during the set. An example pattern of doubles play is as follows:

Player	Points Served	Service Courts
A	1	Right
C	2, 3	Left-Right
B	4, 5	Left-Right
D	6	Left
	Teams Change Ends of Court	
D	7	Right
A	8, 9	Left-Right
C	10, 11	Left-Right
B	12	Left

If Needed, Teams Again Change Ends and Start Rotation Over

The 7-of-12 tie-breaker is a little more complicated and potentially takes more time, since a player must win by two points. Both the 9- and 12-point tie-breakers have obvious strengths and weaknesses, but there is general agreement within the tennis establishment today that a tie-breaking format is needed.

In addition to conventional scoring and tie-breaking procedures, tennis players may also wish to use VASSS, no-ad or the pro-set scoring. VASSS stands for the Van Alen Simplified Scoring System. James Van Alen, a tennis enthusiast and past president of the Tennis Hall of Fame in Newport, Rhode Island, devised a scoring system that is played point by point up to 21 or 31 points, which is the equivalent of a match. In an effort to simplify the scoring and speed up the game, points are accumulated and counted one at a time (1, 2, 3, 4, etc.), and the set score may be either 21 or 31, depending on the preference of the players. Should the score be tied at either 20–20 or 30–30, the match goes into an eight-point overtime with the players serving alternately. Otherwise, the first player to reach 31 points (21 points in shorter version) wins, assuming that the player is ahead by at least two points. In a normal VASSS match, player A serves the first five points, then player B serves the next five points. After the completion of each 10-point segment, the players switch ends of the court.

A pro-set is completed when one player wins at least eight games, based on conventional scoring and is ahead by at least two games.

Another rather popular scoring procedure is the no-ad system, or the "sudden death" method of scoring. The no-ad system eliminates long deuce games, and for that reason, it is widely accepted at all levels of tennis. The first player to win four points wins the game. If the score is tied at 3–3, the receiver is allowed to decide if the seventh or game point should be served to the right or left court. Instead of the conventional scoring (love, 15, 30, 40), a simple point system (1, 2, 3, 4) is used. Should a no-ad set be tied at 6–6, a conventional tie-breaking procedure is implemented.

Players keep their own score in tennis unless they are in tournament play. It is the server's responsibility to call out the score before serving each point. Utilizing this approach, any confusion that may arise can be cleared up before the next point has been completed.

Etiquette and Safety

Tennis is a sport with a proud tradition and a strong code of ethics. Consequently, good sportsmanship is expected of players as they make their calls in recreational play. Even in tournament play, officials are volunteers and thus deserve a special respect for serving in that capacity. Every competitor in tennis is expected to give a 100-percent effort in quest of victory, but not at all costs. Always treat an opponent with trust and respect. Realize that your opponent is not your enemy but a fellow tennis player with a common competitive interest. Regardless of the outcome of the match, be courteous and never allow a simple win or loss to detract from the enjoyment and true spirit of the competition.

Numerous written and unwritten rules of etiquette and safety exist for tennis. You will find that the game is more rewarding and safer if you observe the following basic guidelines:

1. When you make arrangements to play tennis, be there on time. If an emergency occurs, try to contact your opponent beforehand, or at least leave word at the court if possible.

2. Always wear appropriate playing attire, and remember that removing a shirt is normally unacceptable, even for tanning purposes or for coping with extreme conditions of heat and humidity.

3. At the minimum, bring to each match a racket, balls that are in good playing condition, and a towel for removing perspiration. Other accessories are optional. Many avid tennis players take two or more rackets with them in case a string breaks.

4. When you arrive at the court, always try to greet your opponent in a friendly manner with a handshake and a smile.

5. Before warming up, check the height of the net (racket's length plus width of racket head) and clear the court of foreign objects or debris.

6. Be considerate of other tennis players, and do not interrupt play when going to or from your court or while warming up.

7. After a warmup period of 10 to 15 minutes, spin the racket for choice of serve. The winner of the spin has the choice of serving or receiving, with the opponent selecting side of court. Be aware that warming up often involves a wide variety of shots, including the serve. Take your time and warm up thoroughly, realizing that some tennis players require a little more time than others. Also, try to hit the ball back to your opponent each time. Nothing is more aggravating than to have to chase balls excessively during the warmup period.

8. Stray balls are common in tennis, so do not become angry if a ball should roll onto your court during the warmup period or the actual competition. If a ball should roll from your court onto another, be courteous and wait until the point is completed in the other court, and always acknowledge the return with a "thank you."

9. When preparing to serve, always have two balls in your possession. Many players feel more comfortable with three balls in their possession (one in a pocket), which is totally acceptable. Before each serve, make sure the receiver is ready either by holding the balls in the air or giving a simple head shake. Serving before the opponent is ready is poor sportsmanship and is unnecessary.

10. After each serve, again collect at least two balls and verbally announce the score before serving the next point. It is both against the rules and in poor taste to step on or over the baseline

before the ball is hit. The rule infraction is called a "foot fault." Make sure your lead foot is behind the baseline before each service attempt.

11. As a receiver, do not stall or intentionally distract the server. If a served ball does not hit in the proper service court, it is the receiver's responsibility to call a fault. Do so quickly, either verbally or with a hand signal. Pointing the index finger up or to the side indicates that a ball failed to land in the proper service court. Holding the hand flat with the palm down means just the opposite. Many players verbalize their calls (long, wide, out, etc.) on balls that land outside the court, which is an acceptable practice. Any ball that is returned with no response is automatically assumed to be still in play. Moreover, any serve that is a fault should not be returned. Either let the ball bounce past you, or hit it into the net. Making a habit of returning fault serves is extremely discourteous. If you are unsure of a call, you may either ask your opponent for his/her opinion, call it "in," or request that the point be replayed. Just remember that it is your responsibility to make the correct calls. When in doubt, many tennis players let a questionable point stand as a gesture of sportsmanship.

12. Verbal comments after the completion of a point are acceptable as long as they are positive in nature. Complimenting an opponent's shot selection with a "good shot," "well done," or a "good rally" is part of being a good sport. Verbal comments that are negative or emotional outbursts have no place in tennis. Think what you want to, but only verbalize the positive. Otherwise, do not say anything.

13. After a match, congratulate your opponent both verbally and with a handshake. Stress the positive parts of the competition, and do not offer any excuses if you lose. Regardless of the outcome, maintain an attitude of sportsmanship and walk off the court with your head held high, realizing that you gave it your best in an enjoyable, competitive game. Remember, there is always a winner and loser and a next time.

14. Leave the court where you just played in good playing condition. Any empty cans, lids or other trash should be removed from the court. Vacate the court soon after the completion of the match. Save the game discussion for the sidelines, because that allows others to start their play on time.

Not only is the conduct of a player important to the integrity of the game, but the behavior of spectators is also an important factor. Watching a competitive tennis match can be a most enjoyable experience and is encouraged. However, even as a spectator, you have certain rules of etiquette to follow, guidelines that are both written and unwritten. Unfortunately, improper spectator conduct can affect a player's concentration and even influence the outcome of a match. By acting as a spectator the way you would want others to act if you were playing, you help ensure that the experience is a satisfying one for all concerned. The more important guidelines for good spectatorship follow.

1. Normally, bleachers are provided for tennis spectators. You should never sit on or around the actual court unless you have an official function. If bleachers are not available, find a safe place far enough from the court so you will not interfere with play, yet close enough to feel a part of the competition.

2. Applause is encouraged, but be very careful about your timing. Good play should be recognized and applauding is an acceptable display of emotion in tennis, but only after the point has been completed. Applauding, yelling or making any loud noise during a rally is frowned upon in tennis circles and will certainly not be appreciated by the tennis players. Booing or other types of negative emotional behavior is completely unacceptable.

3. The noise level should be kept at a minimum during actual play. If you talk, which is discouraged, keep it at a whisper.

4. Do not talk to the players unless spoken to first or possibly between sets. Do not ask the players the score or engage in other trivial conversation. Allow the players to concentrate.

5. If there are officials or umpires, allow them to do their job without verbal abuse. If you do not agree with a call, which often happens, keep it to yourself. To second-guess their decision verbally, even though they are in a better position to make the call and probably have vastly more experience viewing tennis, is an inexcusable breach against the sport's traditional code of ethics.

II

Learning the Strokes

GRIPPING THE RACKET

A mechanically sound grip of the racket assures that the racket face is horizontal when contact is made with the ball. The racket should be held firmly during the swing and especially at the time of impact. Caution should be taken to avoid holding the racket too tightly. Necessary grip changes are more easily accomodated when the throat of the racket is held with the non-racket hand.

The common grip for hitting a forehand stroke is the Eastern forehand. The proper hand position on the racket can be likened to a handshake. The "V" formed by the thumb and index finger is placed slightly to the left of center of the top plate of the racket. Figures 4 and 5 indicate the proper "V" location for the various grips in tennis.

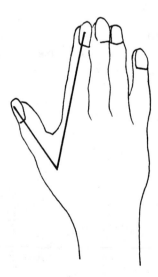

Fig. 4. "V" formed by thumb and index finger.

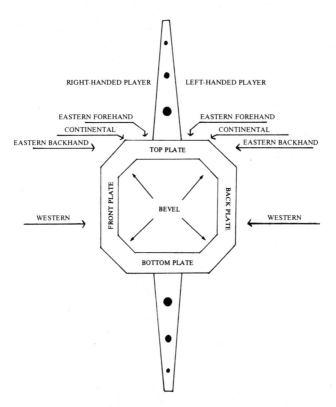

Fig. 5. "V" location for various racket grips along with labeling of racket butt.

In the Eastern forehand grip, the thumb rests against the middle finger. To promote proper leverage in the grip, the position of the index finger is similar to that of a "trigger finger" in shooting sports. A bad habit of some beginners is to point the index finger toward the racket head. Right-handed novices also tend to shift the grip to the right, which means the racket face is tilted to the left, causing balls to be hit into the net.

The bulk of the hand is in back of the racket handle in the Eastern forehand grip, enabling the racket to essentially become an extension of the wrist. Only three knuckles of the gripping hand should be visible to the player: the knuckles of the thumb, index finger and middle finger nearest the palm. The butt or flat end of the racket handle and the lower part of the hand at the base of the grip should be relatively flush, as opposed to a portion of the racket handle protruding beyond the grip of the hand or the end of the racket being cupped inside the palm.

The Eastern backhand is routinely used for hitting backhand strokes. From the Eastern forehand position, a right-handed player makes a one-quarter turn of the racket, which locates the "V" in the middle of the bevel immediately to the left of the plate where the Eastern forehand "V" is placed. In this grip, the bulk of the hand is on top of the racket handle. The

21

thumb can either be diagonally placed across the back of the racket handle or extended up the handle toward the racket head for additional support.

A two-hand backhand grip has grown in popularity over the last decade. For this stroke, the dominant hand assumes either the Eastern forehand or Continental grip, while the non-dominant hand is located above and against the dominant hand. The "V" of the non-dominant hand is located on the same bevel as the dominant hand, and the thumb rests against the index finger. The two-hand grip is reputedly superior to the regular Eastern backhand for promoting power and control in the execution of the stroke.

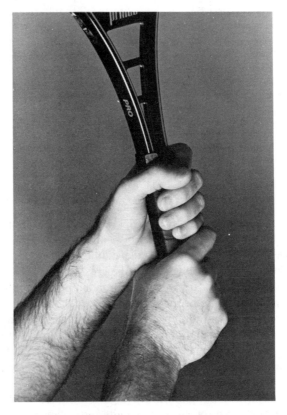

Fig. 6. Two-hand backhand of right-handed player utilizing Continental grip.

The Continental grip can be used for performing all types of tennis strokes. The location of the "V" formed by the thumb and index finger is between those of the Eastern forehand and backhand. Since a player does not have to change grips, valuable time is saved in preparing to hit a ball. As a result, use of the Continental grip is particularly advantageous in doubles play and for hitting volley strokes.

There are other positive features of the Continental grip. A natural slice spin is imparted to the ball when it is utilized. Low bouncing balls are easier to stroke with this grip. Greater control of shot placement is promoted, as the grip allows some additional wrist movement. Since shot placement is improved with the Continental grip, it is recommended for use on the serve once a player reaches an intermediate level of play. By this time, most players have developed a sufficient measure of grip strength to properly execute strokes with the grip. The Continental grip is also suitable for hitting two-handed backhand strokes. The "V" of the non-racket hand is placed on the same bevel as the racket hand.

Power is reduced on strokes performed with the Continental grip due to the natural slice spin placed on the ball. Also, high bouncing balls are difficult to hit when this grip is employed.

Picking a racket up off the floor places the hand in the correct Western grip position. Even though some raw beginners are able to control the racket better with the Western grip, few tennis authorities advocate its use because of the bad habits it produces in stroke mechanics. The grip is simply too mechanically unsound for use in higher level play. However, use of the Western grip does produce much topspin on the ball and enables high bouncing balls to be hit more easily.

More accomplished players tend to favor the Eastern forehand grip for hitting forehand shots and the Continental grip for performing backhand shots. The Eastern forehand grip promotes a more powerful stroke, while the Continental grip enhances stroke control. Employment of this combination will help facilitate your progress toward playing tennis at maximum proficiency.

READY POSITION

Gripping the racket properly is not the only fundamental that must be applied during the preparatory phase for stroking the ball. When anticipating an opponent's return, the assumption of what is known as the "ready position," a body position used in many sports, is another necessary preliminary action. This position effectively promotes movement in any direction and helps contribute to potent ball contact. The knees are bent, with the feet spread slightly further than shoulder width, while the back is kept fairly straight but leaning forward to a small degree. The head is facing the opponent, and the racket is held in both hands in front of the body, with the non-racket hand grasping the throat of the racket (Figure 7).

Despite the importance of positioning the body properly in readiness for an oncoming ball, situations arise in fast-paced tennis play whereby lack of time prohibits a player from assuming the anticipatory ready position. This circumstance frequently occurs when players must prepare to stroke the ball from a forecourt position.

Fig. 7. Ready position.

ANALYSIS OF TENNIS STROKES

Fundamental mechanics of the serve, forehand, two-hand backhand, lob, overhead and volley strokes are presented in this section. These strokes are specific applications and adaptations of the general principles that apply to the mechanics of striking. In all striking activities (batting, kicking, racquetball, etc.), the body acts as a system of linked segments. Imagine a group of children playing "Crack the Whip." When everyone has joined hands, the first child begins to move, pulls the second one and so forth down the line. To make the whip "crack," however, the first child must slow down or stop. As the first link in the chain slows, his/her momentum is passed through the chain to the second child, who accelerates. When the second child slows down, his/her momentum is passed to the third in line and so on.

In much the same way the momentum produced in the body link system is passed from the legs to the trunk, to the segments of the arm, and eventually to the racket, producing the velocity of the racket just before contact with the ball. If properly sequenced, this kinetic chain can transfer the momentum of the body and the racket to the tennis ball. A break in the linked chain, however, or a movement that is out of sequence, detracts from the final velocity. This sequence of segmental rotations is an important concept in the production of the high-velocity striking motions of tennis. The sequence begins with the feet and legs, the segments farthest from the racket, then progresses along the chain through the hips, shoulders, upper arm, forearm, hand and racket. As one segment finishes its motion, the next segment begins its acceleration until the whip cracks and the racket strikes the ball. Using this model in analyzing the tennis strokes, it is quite possible for the first few segments (feet, legs and hips) to be moving forward while the last segments (forearm, hand and racket) are still moving backward in preparation for their forward swing.

Serve (Figures 8–25)

At high skill levels, the serve is one of the player's most powerful offensive weapons. The serve must combine speed with accuracy of placement. To serve effectively, a player should learn to vary the pace, placement and spin of the ball and to use the variations strategically.

Preparation

Feet and Legs. Start with the feet in a stride position 1 to 2 feet apart on a line pointing to the service court. The weight may be on the front foot or balanced between the feet. As the racket is brought back, the legs flex slightly at the knees (Figures 8–14).

Body Action. As the backswing progresses, the hips and shoulders rotate backward and the weight is shifted to the rear foot (Figures 15–17).

Ball and Racket Arm. The ball is tossed straight up, without spin. It should be released at about shoulder height and should rise only slightly above the point at which it will be struck (Figures 8–10). The racket and racket arm are brought up in back of the body, and as the racket reaches its maximum height, the elbow begins to bend (Figure 14). The elbow continues to bend but is kept at a high level, not dropping below the shoulder. The racket head drops behind the back (Figures 19–20) as the elbow begins its forward swing.

Forward Swing

Feet and Legs. The legs begin the forward and upward motion as the weight is transferred from the rear foot to the front foot. As the weight is shifted to the front foot, the legs extend (Figures 18–20).

Body Action. As the feet and legs shift the body weight forward, first the hips, then the upper trunk and shoulders move forward and rotate forward like a spring uncoiling. The non-racket shoulder drops so that the racket shoulder can reach higher (Figures 19–21).

Racket Arm. As the forward rotation of the trunk and shoulder is completed, the elbow of the racket arm begins to swing forward (Figures 19–21), while the racket itself continues down to reach the so-called "back scratch" position seen in Figure 20. The elbow continues forward and the forearm, wrist and eventually the racket follow in the whiplike motion described above. By Figure 21, the forward motion of the elbow has slowed, allowing the acceleration of the forearm and racket (Figures 21–22).

Ball Contact

Contact between racket and ball is made at as high a point as possible. The legs, body, racket arm and racket should be nearly fully extended and reaching up for the ball (Figure 22). A good player is able to use at least two types of serves, the flat serve and the slice serve.

For a flat serve, the line of the racket swing should be toward the service box, and the racket face, at contact, should be perpendicular to the line of intended flight. For a ball hit at a reasonable velocity, only the tallest of players is able to hit a truly flat serve. Unless the point of contact is 8 feet or more above the court, a flat serve will bounce too deep to be legal. Most players who use the flat serve put a small amount of spin on the ball, which allows it to cross the net and still bounce in the service court. The spin is caused by hitting slightly across the ball from the inside out and is a natural result of the trunk rotation and racket swing from behind the body.

The slice serve is executed so that the ball toss is a little farther forward and a little more to the right. The inside-to-outside line of swing is greater than for the flat serve, and the direction of swing is off to the right of the line of ball flight. The racket face must still be perpendicular to the line of ball flight to get the correct direction. It is the line of the swing, not the angle of the racket face, that gives the ball its spin. The line of swing of the racket head should be about 15 to 25 degrees to the right of the ball's line of flight for the slice serve (Figures 21–23).

At ball contact, the player should have a firm grip on the racket. The speed of the served ball is dependent on several things, including the speed of the racket, the firmness of the grip and the physical properties of the ball, racket and strings. A good serving motion will generate sufficient racket speed for a reasonably fast serve. The physical properties of the ball, racket and strings are set ahead of time, but the firmness of the grip at contact will influence the speed of the hit ball. If the grip is not firm, part of the force transmitted to the ball from the racket at contact is lost or "taken up" by the hand and forearm. On off-center hits, if the grip is not firm, the racket face may turn in the hand, resulting in a misdirected hit.

Follow-through

The follow-through is generally down and across the body to the left. It will vary somewhat according to the type of serve (Figures 23–25). Actually, the follow-through does not affect the serve after the ball leaves the racket face, but the follow-through motion does two important things: (1) prevents injury and (2) indicates the actions that preceded it.

In preventing injury, the follow-through provides a long distance through which to slow down the fast-moving body parts. Slowing down a fast-moving arm too quickly can cause injury to the muscles that produce the slowing down. Proper follow-through avoids this possibility by allowing for a gradual slowing down of body parts.

The follow-through also indicates what actually went on during the force-producing portion of the service action. The movements just before and during ball contact take place so quickly that it is not possible to see or even feel what is happening. The slower movements in the follow-through can be good indicators of the direction and speed of the motions during the high-speed phase of the action.

26

Racket Arm. After ball contact, the racket and racket arm swing down and across the body (Figures 23–25). During this time, the arm rotates in toward the body at the shoulder joint. The hand and forearm continue the inward rotation with the thumb of the racket hand pointing downward (Figures 23–25).

Body Action. The shoulders continue to rotate, and the shoulder of the racket arm moves across the body and down. A slight forward bend at the hips at contact and during the follow-through indicates good body action.

Feet and Legs. The force of the serving action brings the right hip forward to facilitate a step into the court.

8   9

Sequence photography was shot with the Canon High Speed F-1 Camera at 14 frames per second.

10

11

12

13

14

15

16

17

18

19

20

21

22

23

24

25

Forehand Drive (Figures 26–39)

Preparation

The backswing begins early, during the time the player is moving to the ball (Figures 26–30). It should be smooth and easy, not hurried.

Feet and Legs. During play in tennis the backswing should be completed as the player moves to the ball. Ideally, the player will be moving forward from the right or rear foot during the hit. By the time the backswing is completed, the weight should be on the rear foot, and the player should have room to step forward into the ball for contact (Figure 31).

Body Action. The entire body, except for the head, should rotate backward during the preparation, and the line of the shoulders should be perpendicular to the net (Figure 31).

Racket and Racket Arm. There are several variations of backswing that can be used successfully to get the racket and arm in proper position for the forward swing. The racket may be brought back with the wrist cocked in a high position, then dropped lower as the forward swing begins. It is probably best for the novice to bring the racket straight back at about hip level, with the shaft of the racket nearly parallel to the ground or pointing only slightly up. The racket arm should be away from the body and bent slightly at the elbow (Figures 26–31).

Forward Swing

Feet and Legs. The forward swing is initiated by a step diagonally forward. The length of the step sideways will vary to allow for adjustments to be made in the distance from the ball. Sometimes during play it will be necessary for this step to be directly to the side, but if at all possible, the step should have a forward component, which can add speed to the hit ball. During the step, the weight is forcefully shifted to the forward foot, with the rear foot actively pushing forward (Figures 33–36). The body is kept low by bending at the knees, not at the waist.

Body Action. As the weight is shifted forward during the step, the entire trunk—hips first, then chest and finally shoulders—turns forward. The trunk should be nearly erect, not bent forward at the waist or hips. The combined action of the step and trunk rotation causes the shoulder of the racket arm to turn and move forward toward the oncoming ball (Figures 34–36). As the shoulder slows (Figures 36–37), the racket and racket arm accelerate forward.

Racket and Racket Arm. The racket and racket arm lag behind the shoulder to produce a whiplike motion (Figures 35–36). The racket arm should be slightly bent at the elbow during the forward swing. In the last portion of the forward swing, the racket head should move from low to high (Figures 35–37). The racket head may drop slightly below the wrist to facilitate the low-to-high forward swing. The fact that the racket is moving up as the ball is hit produces a topspin on the ball. Attempting to produce the topspin by rolling the wrist and forearm over the top of the ball at contact is not advised. Such action does not produce satisfactory topspin, often misdirects the ball (into the net), and can lead to serious injury of the muscles of the forearm.

Ball Contact

Feet and Legs. The body weight is moving forward, so that the weight is on the forward foot at contact.

Body Action. The trunk is moving forward and rotating through ball contact (Figures 36–37).

Racket and Racket Arm. The racket face should be perpendicular to the intended line of flight and approximately parallel to the net at the time of ball contact (Figure 37). The ball should hit the center of the strings, and the grip should be firm to produce a forceful hit. Off-center hits tend to twist the racket in the hand and can cause injury to the forearm muscles. Topspin imparted to the ball should result from the low-to-high forward swing of the racket head. Backspin for a drop shot is produced in a similar manner, except that the swing is from high in back to low in front and the force of the hit is usually less.

Follow-through

Follow-through for the forehand drive is generally up and across the body to the player's left (Figures 37–39).

26   27

28   29

30   31

32   33

34   35

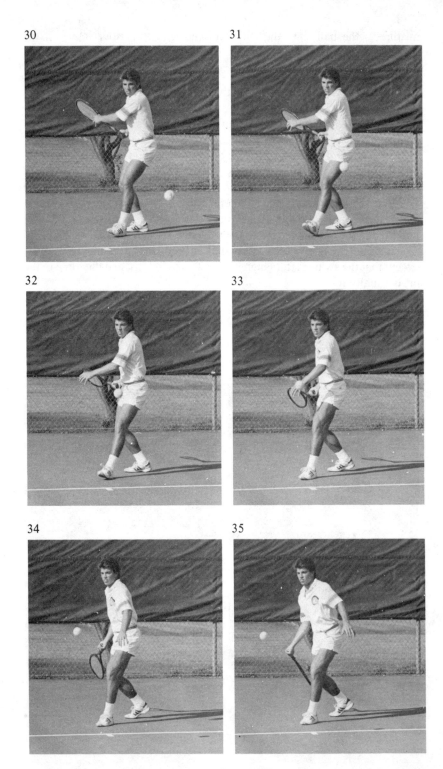

Forehand Lob (Figures 40-45)

To be strategically useful, the forehand lob should be executed to look just like the forehand drive. The backswing and forward swing, up to the point of contact, should be the same as for the drive (Figures 40–43). The change in mechanics that produces the high loft of the lob is that the racket face is turned slightly up just at contact (Figure 44). Often the lob is hit with slightly less force than the drive, but for the shot to be effective, the reduction in force should not be noticeable. To keep the ball in the court, it is better to hit a lob with topspin. Topspin for the lob is produced in the same way as for the drive, by moving the racket head from low to high as the ball is hit (Figures 42–44). The follow-through is again similar to that of the drive, across the body and upward (Figure 45).

40

41

42

43

44

45

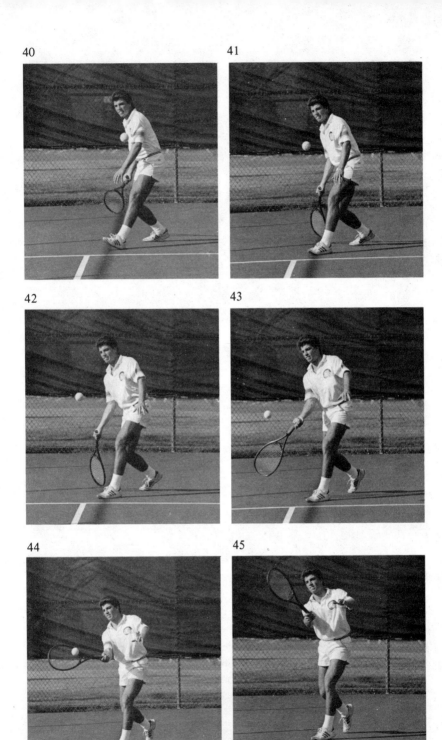

Two-Hand Backhand Drive (Figures 46–55)

The two-hand backhand drive has become popular in recent years because of several advantages that is has over the one-hand backhand drive. Probably the greatest advantage is that a two-hand backhand tends to protect the muscles and joints of the arm. In addition, it provides a natural topspin, which allows a more forceful hit to remain in-bounds. Returning a topspin ball is somewhat more difficult than returning either a backspin ball or a ball with no spin. A topspin ball drops at a sharper angle than a ball with no spin and rebounds at an angle closer to the ground. A topspin ball can actually pick up velocity on the bounce, so that it seems to hit short and bounce quickly away.

Preparation

As for the forehand drive, the preparation for the backhand begins early (Figures 46–50).

Feet and Legs. As the player moves toward the ball, the weight is shifted to the left or rear foot (Figure 47). The rear foot should be placed so that the player can step forward into the ball for the contact (Figures 47–52).

Body Action. The backswing begins with a backward turn of the hips and trunk, followed by the shoulders (Figures 46–49). The shoulder of the racket arm is lower than the rear shoulder and almost points to the oncoming ball.

Racket and Racket Arms. For the two-hand backhand, the right hand does not switch to a backhand grip. The left hand grasps the racket just above the right hand in what is similar to a forehand grip for the left hand. Both hands take the racket back to a low position at the end of the backswing (Figure 50).

Forward Swing

Feet and Legs. The body weight is moved forward by a step diagonally forward toward the oncoming ball. The knee of the front leg is bent to keep the body low. The rear foot actively pushes forward to transfer the force of the body weight to the ball.

Body Action. As the front foot is planted in its forward step, the body begins to rotate forward (Figures 50–52). The muscles of the hips and trunk turn the body and shoulders forward toward the ball. The whole body is moving forward.

Racket and Racket Arms. The forward swing of the racket is initiated in the shoulders, followed by the elbow and hands. As the racket is brought forward, the racket head is gradually raised (Figures 50–53), so that topspin can be imparted to the ball as the racket contacts the ball.

Ball Contact

Racket and Racket Arms. The plane of the racket face should be parallel to the net and perpendicular to the ball's line of intended flight

(Figure 53) at contact. The racket head will be moving up at contact due to the low-to-high path of the forward swing. The grip should be firm, and the ball should contact the center of the racket face.

Follow-through

The follow-through for the two-hand backhand is generally up and across the body to the player's right (Figures 54–55). The trunk rotates forward, and the rear foot comes forward for a smooth return to the ready position.

46

47

48

49

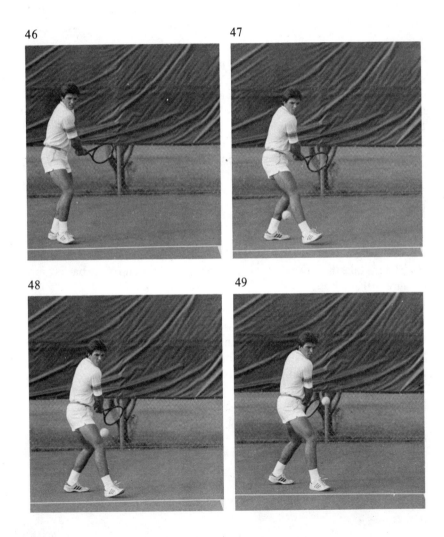

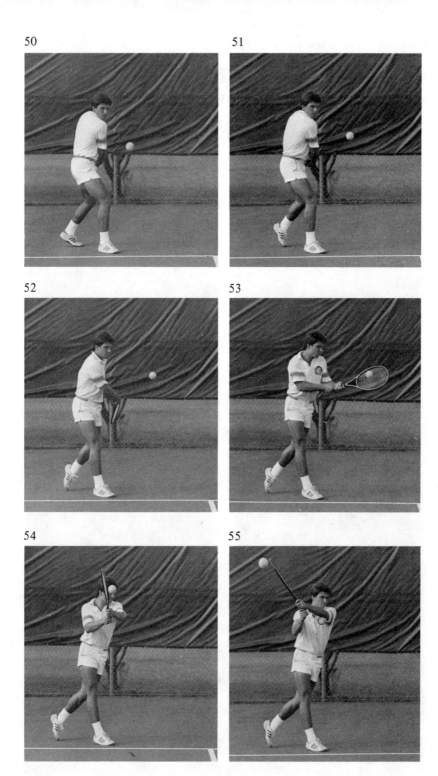

50

51

52

53

54

55

Backhand Lob (Figures 56–61)

Like the forehand lob, the backhand lob, to be used successfully, must look like the backhand drive. The backswing and forward swing for the lob are the same as for the drive, up to the point of contact (Figures 56–60). At contact, the racket face is tilted slightly upward (Figure 60) to give the ball the loft needed for a lob. As in the backhand drive, topspin is a natural result of the low-to-high path of the swing (Figures 58–60). The follow-through is similar to that seen in the drive, up and across the body to the right (Figure 61).

56   57

58   59

Overhead (Figures 62–75)

The overhead or smash is an offensive stroke used to return a lob, especially a short lob. The overhead is very similar to the serve in terms of the mechanics of the stroke. There are, however, some essential differences. First, the ball is not tossed straight up, as in the serve, but is falling toward the player attempting the smash. This means that it will almost always be necessary to back up to hit the overhead, and this footwork can be the hardest part of the stroke. Second, since the shot is hit from a point closer to the net, the ball may be contacted farther in front of the player than a serve normally is, and the ball may be hit without spin.

Preparation

Feet and Legs. The player preparing to hit an overhead is nearly always forced to move backward to get into position for the shot. To move backward quickly, the right foot should drop back immediately and sidestep into position. Sidestepping enables the player to turn the body sideways to the net as he/she moves back. Once the player has reached a position from which the ball can be hit, the weight is shifted to the right or back foot. The knee of the rear leg bends slightly in preparation for the forward and upward swing (Figures 62–66).

Body Action. As in the service motion, the hips, trunk and shoulders rotate backward so that the left side faces the net. The body weight is fully on the rear foot. The shoulder of the non-racket arm is raised, while the shoulder of the racket arm is dropped. It is often suggested that the player point to the oncoming ball with the non-racket hand. While this is not necessary, it does facilitate the rotation of the shoulders and the dropping of the racket arm (Figure 67).

Racket and Racket Arm. The racket and racket arm are brought up to the side and back in preparation for the overhead. Compared to the service motion, the backswing for the overhead is somewhat abbreviated, although the motion ends in a similar "back scratch" position (Figure 69).

Forward Swing

Feet and Legs. The rear leg straightens and the weight is shifted to the front leg during the forward swing (Figures 69–70).

Body Action. The body action in the overhead is very similar to that seen in the serve. The hips begin the forward rotation, followed by the trunk and shoulders. As the shoulders rotate forward, the shoulder of the racket arm begins to come up while the non-racket shoulder drops. The whole body is moving forward as the weight shifts from the rear to the front foot (Figures 69–71).

Racket and Racket Arm. The action of the racket and racket arm for the overhead is similar to the arm actions during the flat serve. As the shoulder rotation slows, the elbow of the racket arm begins to swing forward (Figure 69). The racket lags behind the elbow and hand (Figures 69–70) until the elbow extends and whips the racket to the extended position seen at contact in Figure 71.

Ball Contact

The ball is contacted high above and in front of the right shoulder. Since the player is closer to the net than in the serve, the ball does not have to be contacted as high, and the ball position may be farther in front of the player than for the serve. The racket face may be turned slightly to place the smash to a particular part of the opponent's court. Advanced players may want to add spin to the ball, as in the serve, but accurate placement should be developed first.

Follow-through

Follow-through is down and across the body to the left (Figures 72–75). The body rotation continues, and the weight is carried completely over the forward or left foot.

62

63

64

65

66

67

68

69

70

71

72

73

74

75

Volley (Figures 76–83 and 84–91)

The volley is an offensive shot that is used when the player is near or approaching the net. It is offensive because it is returned more quickly than a ground stroke and because of the large areas of the opponent's court to which it can be hit.

Preparation

Because the player is close to the net, there is less time in the volley to prepare and to hit the ball. The player should be in a good "ready" position, with the feet about shoulder width apart, knees slightly bent, and the weight forward on the toes. The racket is held up in front with both hands. Intermediate and advanced players generally use a Continental grip, so that either a forehand or backhand volley can be hit without changing grips. Beginners usually use the Eastern forehand and change to the backhand grip for a backhand volley.

Footwork. There is little time for footwork when hitting a volley, and yet the player must be prepared to cover a fairly large area to either side. There are two basic patterns of footwork used in the volley, the sidestep and the crossover. The sidestep pattern is used when the player does not have to reach very far to the side to play the ball. It is slightly faster than the crossover but is ineffective if the ball is out of easy reach. In using the sidestep, the player simply steps to the side with the foot nearest the oncoming ball. If time permits, it is advantageous to step forward at the same time.

The crossover step is demonstrated in the backhand volley sequence (Figures 84–91). This pattern is much quicker when the player must reach very far to either side. The weight is shifted to the foot on the ball side (Figure 84), and the opposite foot is brought across and extended toward the oncoming ball (Figures 85–87). Using this technique, the player is able to reach balls wide on either side.

For volleys taken above the waist leg action is similar to that used for ground strokes. For low volleys the bend in the knees is greater. The player hitting a low volley must get the body low by bending at the knees, rather than simply bending forward at the waist.

Body Action. Because the volley must be hit quickly, there is little time for much body action. The player should try to get as much shoulder rotation and forward movement of the trunk as possible in the time available. For more slowly hit balls, the player may be able to make a full shoulder turn and step forward into the shot. When returning a hard-hit ball, there may be no time for any shoulder rotation or forward movement. One advantage to using the crossover step pattern is that it rotates the shoulders.

Racket and Racket Arm. The backswing is limited and varies according to the speed of the oncoming ball. The racket is brought back to a point about even with the shoulder. The wrist should be held firm during the backswing and the forward motion. The racket should be brought to a point slightly higher than where impact will occur.

Forward Swing

Actually, the volley should be a short, crisp punch and not a swing at all. The body moves forward, if time permits. The racket is held firmly with the wrist locked. A short forward motion of the whole arm and racket brings the racket to the ball at contact (Figures 80–82 and 88–90). The player should try to punch through the ball rather than swing at it.

Ball Contact

The racket arm and hand must remain firm during ball contact. The ball should contact the racket in the center of the strings. The face of the racket will be tilted slightly, depending on where the ball is hit relative to the net. For a high volley, the racket face may be tilted down slightly and angled to place the ball to the side. A low volley, hit below the net cord, requires that the racket face be angled up to allow the ball to rebound over the net. A common error, however, is to angle the racket face too much and hit a high, short volley that can be easily returned for a winner by the opponent. A good player will commonly place volleys to open areas of the opponent's court by turning the racket face slightly to one side or the other.

Follow-through

Since the forward motion of the volley is not a swing, there will be little follow-through after the hit. The most important part of the follow-through is to return quickly to the ready position.

76

77

78

79

80

81

82

83

84

85

86

87

88

89

90

91

III

Improving Your Skills

No magic formula exists that will improve a player's game or promote his/her progression from a beginner to an advanced player overnight. Only through regular practice, hard work and concentration can you expect to improve your playing skill. Improvement in playing ability builds confidence. Thus, practice or drill work tends to improve the mental component of a player's game as well as the physical.

At any proficiency level, tennis requires a certain degree of neuromuscular skill, involving such physical skills as coordination, quickness, agility, speed and endurance. Practice will enable you to develop a proper level of physical fitness, or as it is commonly referred to, "to get into shape." Many serious tennis players spend as much, if not more, time practicing the related skills as they do playing competitively.

Stroke repetition and drill work in practice sessions must be systematic and progressive to be effective. Plan your practice sessions with certain objectives in mind, realizing that it is virtually impossible to work on all phases of your tennis game in one session. Remember that skill development takes time, so be patient and give yourself a fair chance to get better at your own pace. Avoid comparing your progress with that of another tennis player, especially at the beginning level. Be assured that serious attention to practice and a good mental attitude is a successful combination that will eventually work for you in your effort to improve.

Tennis instructors often hear the excuse, "But practice is so boring." However, drill work is only tedious and boring if you want it to be. Actually, most avid tennis players agree that drill work can be fun and enjoyable if you follow a few simple guidelines.

1. Do not spend the whole session on one particular drill. Change the drill every five to ten minutes, and slowly increase the variety of drills you are using as your skill increases.

2. Do not attempt a drill that is above your skill level. Be patient and work on drills that you feel comfortable with. As you experience success with a particular drill, proceed to a similar drill involving a higher degree of difficulty.

3. Drill work can be very competitive, especially since you are competing against yourself. Keep a record of your success rate (number, duration, etc.) for each drill, and constantly try to beat yesterday's results.

4. Drills do not have to be done alone. Take a friend and either take turns doing a particular drill or engage in drills that involve two players.

5. Keep in mind that the time you spend in practice will not only improve your tennis ability but will allow you to "burn" calories while having fun. Even though you may be achieving weight control and getting into better physical condition, you may not realize all the positive benefits until later.

To make it easier for the student of tennis, the following drills are presented by particular stroke, progressing from the fundamental beginning level drills to the more demanding advanced drills. Practice drills may involve only one player or two or more. Both individual and group drills are important to the ultimate goal of improving a player's skill level. In each stroke category, the individual drills are presented first, followed by group drills.

RACKET ACQUAINTANCE DRILLS

Racket Air Bounce Drill

Objective. To become familiar with the feel of the racket and tennis ball.

Description. Grip a racket with the Eastern forehand grip and proceed to bounce a tennis ball on the face of the racket while the racket head is parallel to the floor. The ball should make contact in the "sweet spot" or center of the racket face. Try to consecutively bounce the ball off the racket face as many times as possible. The height of the bounce should be between 2 and 3 feet.

General Comments. The height of the bounce should be consistent at first, and the player should try to stand in the same spot. As you progress, you can increase the height of the bounce and add a walking pace to the drill. Once the ball hits the ground, start the drill and your count again.

Racket Dribble Drill

Objective. To become familiar with the feel of the racket and tennis ball.

Description. Grip a racket with an Eastern forehand grip and proceed to dribble a tennis ball on the surface while the racket head is parallel to the floor. The height of the dribble should be level with your waist, and the ball should be making contact in the "sweet spot" or center of the racket face. Remain in the same spot and dribble the ball as many times in succession as possible.

General Comments. As you progress, you can begin to walk while dribbling the ball. Then pick up the pace until you are successfully running and dribbling the tennis ball at the same time.

Both of the racket acquaintance drills can involve a partner. In the racket air bounce drill, two players stand facing each other, approximately 5 feet apart. They proceed to bounce a tennis ball from racket to racket while attempting to control both the height of the air bounce and placement of the ball. Difficulty may be added to the drill by moving farther apart while still controlling both the height and accuracy of the air bounce.

The racket dribble drill involving two players also begins with the pair facing each other, approximately 5 feet apart. They dribble the ball to each other, keeping the bounce waist high while concentrating on both accuracy and velocity of the dribble. Again, if the players move farther apart, the difficulty of the drill increases. The idea behind the drill is to bounce the ball off the ground once, and only once, between racket hits. To add additional difficulty to both drills, the two players may run in a circle while bouncing the ball to each other.

Racket Edge Air Bounce Drill

Objective. To become familiar with the feel of the racket and tennis ball.

Description. Grip a racket with an Eastern forehand grip and proceed to bounce a ball off the edge of the racket head while the head of the racket is held perpendicular to the floor. This drill is identical to the racket air bounce drill except for racket positioning.

General Comments. This is an advanced drill and should only be attempted after successfully completing the previous two racket acquaintance drills.

GROUND STROKE DRILLS — FOREHAND AND BACKHAND

The forehand and backhand ground stroke drills are discussed together, since the two types of drills follow the same basic format. Forehand drills are performed on the right side for right-handed players and the left side for left-handed players. Backhand drills are performed on the left side for right-handed players and on the right side for left-handed players.

Positioning Drill

Objective. To practice correct footwork and body positioning for performing the basic ground strokes.

Description. The mechanics of a ground stroke involve a pivot, step, swing and follow-through. Assuming you are facing the net, the first move is a pivot or turn to the side of the ball. The body is now in position to step into or toward the ball with the foot opposite the ball side. As you step into the shot, the racket swing should be initiated so that when your foot contacts the ground, the downswing of the racket has started. The follow-through is a key variable, since it helps determine accuracy and velocity and corrects body positioning after the racket has made contact with the ball.

General Comments. As with all ground stroke drills, this drill should be practiced from both the forehand and backhand side. The drill begins as a step-by-step (one, two, three, four) maneuver, but after many practice trials, it becomes a fluid, smooth motion. The idea is to position your body in the right place at the right time during the actual ground stroke. The drill should first be done without a ball. Once the total motion becomes comfortable, take a ball in your non-racket hand and bounce it (as you start your pivot) at a point where you think you would normally make contact. When you initially involve a ball in this drill, do not worry about placement or speed. Concentrate first on a fluid motion, proper stepping distance and racket head positioning upon contact. Once you have worked out the basic mechanics of the forehand and backhand swings, try to hit the ball over the net into the opposite court. Also, work on accuracy and placement before considering the speed or velocity of the shot. Be patient and realize that success in applying the forehand mechanics tends to come long before proficiency with the backhand. That is normal, so do not become discouraged.

If you wish to involve another person in this drill, have your partner stand 20 to 25 feet in front of you and bounce the ball to your forehand and backhand sides. This allows you to practice body positioning for an oncoming opponent return.

Wall Rally Drill

Objective. To practice the basic ground strokes while improving ball control ability.

Description. Stand approximately 25 feet away from a wall and proceed to hit forehand and backhand ground strokes, with the forehand strokes being hit first. The drill should be initiated by bouncing a ball to your forehand side, followed by a fluid swinging motion (pivot, step, swing and follow-through). Stop the ball after it bounces off the wall and again initiate the forehand with a bounce and swing. Continue this procedure until you feel comfortable with your swing and you are able to consistently hit the wall.

After a period of practice, you should attempt to hit consecutive forehand shots to the wall while not worrying about the number of bounces the ball might take between shots. As you progressively improve, concentrate on the height of the ball when it makes contact with the wall. Place a mark 3 feet high on the wall to simulate the regular net height, and try to hit the ball consistently over the mark. Make every effort to return the ball after only one bounce, which means footwork and body movement become important maneuvers. Be sure to allow equal time for practicing the backhand, using the same procedure as that used on the forehand side.

General Comments. A distance of 25 feet is recommended for beginners, but as a player improves, the distance from the wall should be increased to at least 39 feet, since that is the regulation distance from the baseline to the net. Since the primary objective is to improve a player's ability to consistently and accurately hit ground strokes, each player should keep count of the number of consecutive ground strokes that are properly returned (that is, strokes where the ball is hit after one bounce and strikes the wall above the 3-foot mark). Even beginners eventually realize that a ball that strikes 10 feet high on the wall is not a desirable return, since it has no chance of landing in the opponent's court (unless it is a lob shot). Try to keep the ball between 3 and 6 feet high on the wall if possible.

You are strongly urged to spend as much time on the backhand as the forehand, and you should realize that the success rate will be significantly less on the backhand at the beginning. It is a good idea to alternate forehand and backhand strokes during the rally, but only after both strokes have been practiced thoroughly and separately.

Partner Rally Drill

Objective. To improve ground stroke control while concentrating on the correct court movement and body positioning.

Description. The players should stand on opposite sides of the court approximately 3 feet behind the baseline at the center mark. One player initiates the drill by hitting a forehand shot over the net into the partner's backcourt, ensuring that the ball bounces back to the baseline. The partner takes a forehand position and returns the ball to the backcourt so it will bounce past the baseline. Consecutive forehand shots should be hit, with each player attempting to hit the ball deep and to the drill partner's forehand side. Once the forehand ground stroke has been thoroughly practiced, then switch to the backhand side and follow the same procedure.

As players progress in consistency and accuracy, the partner rally drill should continue, but with the players using only one side of the court. This variation is called the one-sided partner rally drill. The players again take a position behind opposite baselines, but instead of stationing themselves in the center of the court, they take a position in the center of either the left or right half of the court. They proceed to rally the ball through the use of either a forehand or backhand stroke while attempting to keep the ball on only one half of the court. This variation of the rally drill stresses the importance of shot placement.

Another variation is referred to as the cross-court partner rally drill. Again, both players take a position behind the baseline on opposite sides of the court, with each player standing to the far right or diagonally opposite each other. They proceed to rally, using primarily the forehand stroke and attempting to hit the ball diagonally across court each time. After a period of practice, they move to the far left, stay behind the baseline and proceed to rally, this time using the backhand stroke.

General Comments. In the partner rally drill and the variations, the ball should always be played on the first bounce, and each player should make every effort to hit the ball back to the other with as much accuracy as possible. A good way to add excitement and fun to the drills is to keep score of successful placements. Since the objective is to improve both accuracy and consistency, a player receives one point each time the ball goes over the net and lands in the proper area. The first player to score 10, 20, or whatever point total is agreed upon, is the winner. Incidentally, the initial bounce and hit does not count as a point.

As a player gains confidence in the ground strokes, the speed or velocity of the return gradually increases. Unfortunately, if the speed factor is stressed too soon, it can slow the progress of the skill development pertaining to the basic mechanics of the ground strokes. Consistency is probably the most important ingredient in drill work, with placement and accuracy being a close second, especially for beginning and intermediate players. "Big hitters" are normally advanced tennis players who have years of experience. In all probability, they did not start out that way. Much practice and patience are required to reach that level, since consistency and accuracy in hitting the ball must be developed before stroke velocity.

Players are strongly recommended to reposition themselves immediately after returning the ball during ground stroke drills, especially when performing the partner rally drill. Correct court positioning is very important to successful tennis and should be emphasized even in drill work.

SERVICE DRILLS

Service Toss Drill

Objective. To improve the consistency of the service toss, since an accurate and consistent toss is a key component of the serve.

Description. This drill may be practiced anywhere, but the ideal position is standing just behind the baseline while facing the net. This adds realism to the drill, since you are practicing from the normal service area. Place your racket head at a spot that represents the location where a tossed serve should land. The preferred spot is slightly in front of the baseline and in line with the right shoulder. A right-handed player should take a ball in the left hand and toss it in the air as if to initiate a serve. Pay particular attention to the height of the ball and the accuracy of the toss in relationship to the body. If the toss is done correctly, the ball should land on the racket head and bounce back up to you. Take your time and continue to toss the ball until you have developed the required consistency.

General Comments. An accurate and consistent service toss requires a great deal of practice to develop, so do not become discouraged if you do not succeed immediately. Once you feel comfortable with your toss, you might want to add the normal body rotation that is also an integral part of the serve, taking into account that you are practicing this rotation without a racket in your hand.

Service Form Drill

Objective. To coordinate the total body rotation with the ball toss while actually serving the ball, without being concerned about the placement or speed of the serve.

Description. Stand 5 to 7 feet away from a fence or net and practice the serve. Draw an imaginary baseline and work on the ball toss, body rotation, arm extension, and hitting the ball as you would during a regular game. Avoid any concern about how high the ball hits on the net or fence in the early stages. With practice, players eventually become more comfortable with the total service motion, and only then should work on service placement be initiated.

General Comments. The tennis serve is a difficult stroke to master, so be patient and allow yourself plenty of practice time. The serve is a very important part of tennis, and for that reason, many players at all skill levels spend a great deal of time practicing the serve.

Half-Court Serve Drill

Objective. Once the basic body mechanics of the serve have been practiced, service placement is the next important hurdle. This drill allows a player to concentrate on ball placement from a position closer to the net than normal.

Description. Stand just behind the service line and immediately to the right of the center service line. Once in position, proceed to serve a ball diagonally into the right service court. Placement is important, so try to consistently serve within the boundaries of the right service court. Forget about the speed of the serve until you have achieved consistent placement. As you improve, add a faster body rotation and arm swing to the service motion. This promotes an increase in service velocity. When you have thoroughly practiced the right service court serve, then move to the left of the center service line and serve diagonally into the left service court. Be sure to practice an equal amount of time from both the right and left sides.

General Comments. By initially standing at the service line, each player should experience a higher rate of success, which allows him/her to concentrate more on placement and speed while gaining confidence in performing the serve. As service ability improves, the distance from the net to the server should be increased until the baseline is reached.

Serve and Return Drill

Objective. To improve a player's serving ability.

Description. Stand just behind the baseline and immediately to the right of the center service line, just as you would if it were the first serve of an actual game. Serve the ball diagonally into the right service court, concentrating on both the placement and speed of the serve. After practicing from the right side, move to the left of the center service line and continue to work on your serving consistency. This is a good time to work on serves toward an imaginary opponent's forehand and backhand sides, as well as for practicing spin serves. Remember that serving to an empty service court is different than serving to an opponent.

Once you feel comfortable serving to an empty court, have your partner take a proper service return position and stroke the ball back over the net after each serve. The drill then becomes valuable for both players, as it becomes a serve and return drill. After thoroughly practicing your serve, switch roles and become the returner. Avoid the temptation to keep score. Just concentrate on the serve and service return.

General Comments. This is an excellent drill for a server, regardless of his/her skill level. The drill promotes service consistency, improves forehand and backhand placement, and allows for the practice of spin serves. The partner is also given the opportunity to work on positioning for the service return along with return placement.

Advanced drills for the serve simply involve a player serving from the baseline while working on such things as precise placement, spin and the speed of the serve. Most skilled tennis players would agree that proficiency in serving is attained only through much hard work and concentration.

VOLLEY DRILLS

Wall Volley Drill

Objective. To develop the hitting technique for the volley shot.

Description. Stand approximately 5 feet from a wall and proceed to continuously hit a ball against the wall, concentrating initially on the forehand volley. With any volley shot, it is important that you follow the flight of the ball until it makes contact with your racket. In other words, keep your eyes on the ball and try to have the ball consistently make contact with the racket at the "sweet spot." Once you feel comfortable with the forehand, switch to the backhand and again hit volley shots continuously against the wall. As you improve, move back from the wall until you are consistently hitting both the forehand and backhand volley shots from a distance of 10 feet.

General Comments. A common mistake with any volley shot is to overswing or try to "power" the ball over the net. Work on a smooth, fluid swing while concentrating on accuracy. Do not be concerned about ball velocity until later. As your skill improves, alternate forehand and backhand volleys and gradually increase the speed of the shot.

Stationary Volley Drill

Objective. To improve the consistency and accuracy of the volley shot.

Description. Stand between 5 and 7 feet from the net, facing it and straddling the center service line. Have your partner stand at the service line on the opposite side of the net and throw a tennis ball to your forehand side. Attempt to hit a volley shot over the net while concentrating on hand-eye coordination and ball-racket contact. Avoid any concern about ball placement or speed. After thoroughly practicing the forehand volley, go to the backhand, staying 5 to 7 feet from the net and in the center of the court.

After some improvement, increase the distance from the net to 10 to 12 feet and continue to practice both forehand and backhand shots. You should eventually work your way back to the service line, a distance of 21 feet from the net.

General Comments. Once you have developed hitting consistency with the volley shot, placement is the next important objective. Placing the volley return at an angle, either to the right or left, is usually preferred. Gradually increase the tempo of your swing, and speed of the return will increase accordingly.

As you gain some confidence in your volley stroke, it is a good idea to have your partner hit a ground stroke to you instead of simply throwing the ball. This adds a little more speed to the oncoming ball and requires some movement on your part in order to obtain proper positioning.

An excellent variation of the stationary volley drill involves two players hitting a ball continuously over the net without allowing the ball to hit the playing surface. In the partner volley drill, each player stands facing the net, approximately 5 feet away, and proceeds to volley the ball back and forth, concentrating on consistency. As progress is made, the players move farther from the net until they have reached the service line.

Moving Volley Drill

Objective. To improve a player's ability to set up and hit a volley shot in a simulated game situation.

Description. As in the previously discussed stationary volley drill, start at a position 5 to 7 feet away from the net and in the middle of the court. Have your partner hit ground strokes from the baseline to both your forehand and backhand side, varying the speed and height of the ball. Instead of hitting the ball directly to you, he/she should hit it at least 8 to 10 feet to each side. This way you will be forced to move to the shot, as opposed to standing in the center of the court.

As you progress, increase the distance from the net until you have at least reached the service line, a distance of 21 feet. Concentrate on shot consistency and placement. Speed is developed naturally as confidence in hitting the volley shot is increased.

General Comments. Proper positioning is an important prerequisite for the successful return of any tennis shot, especially the volley. React to the ball as soon as it leaves the opponent's racket, if not before. Based on the body position of your opponent, you can often determine the angle of the return or the shot selection ahead of time. Body language in tennis varies from player to player, but a correct interpretation of an opponent's movement definitely gives a player an advantage in shot anticipation and reaction time. Drill work provides a player the opportunity to study a partner's body language, which can be later applied against a real opponent. Take full advantage of this opportunity during drills such as the moving volley drill.

Serve and Volley Drill

Objective. To develop the volley shot during forward movement or while "rushing" the net.

Description. Many tennis players have developed a playing philosophy that includes a serve, rapid forward movement to the net and a volley return. This style of play places more pressure on the receiver during the return of serve, and it also stresses the importance of developing a consistent and well-placed volley shot for the server. The serve and volley drill should help you develop the technique and confidence for hitting the volley return while moving in a forward direction.

Stand at the baseline facing the net, and have your partner stand at the opposite baseline and face the net. Initiate the drill by going through the motions of a serve, without using a ball (shadow serve). Continue toward the net after you have completed your service motion and stay in the middle of the court. After you complete your service motion, your partner should hit a ground stroke from the baseline for you to return with a volley shot. You are encouraged to first work on forehand volley returns, then shift to backhand returns, followed by an alternation of sides or a sequence selected at random by your partner.

General Comments. Concentrate on moving to the net rapidly, yet under control. Keep your eyes on the ball from the time it leaves your partner's racket, and work on shot consistency and angle placement. Be aware that a volley shot is considered an intermediate level shot. As a general rule, beginning tennis players should concentrate on the racket acquaintance, ground stroke (forehand and backhand) and service drills, while intermediate and advanced players should work on the shot variations such as the volley, smash, lob, drop and half volley.

OVERHEAD/SMASH DRILL

Objective. To improve a player's stroke technique in performing the overhead smash shot.

Description. The overhead, or smash, is very similar to the serve as far as body movement and positioning is concerned. They are both offensive power strokes that require precise timing and good judgment, and both are important to the overall game of tennis.

An overhead may be hit one of two ways, either after a bounce or directly in the air before the bounce. It should definitely be practiced both ways.

Take a position in the center of the court about 5 to 7 feet away from the net, and have your partner throw the ball high and to your forehand side. Concentrate on good arm extension and body rotation, just as you did with the serve. A common beginning mistake with the smash shot is to try to overpower the ball. Initially, strive for a smooth, consistent swing and concentrate on a high contact point for the ball to hit the "sweet spot" of the racket. Disregard placement or speed until you feel comfortable with the full motion of the smash shot. Most players have time to position themselves for a forehand smash because of the height of the ball. Practice the backhand smash along with the forehand, but spend the majority of drill time with the forehand, since at least 90 percent of smashes are hit on the forehand side.

If your partner is capable of hitting a consistently high lob shot for you to smash, that is probably better than attempting to throw the ball. As you get better at hitting the smash shot, speed up your body rotation and arm swing to promote more velocity on the ball. Also, hit angle shots whenever possible, since they create a more difficult return.

Next, take a position at the service line and practice forehand smashes. You should realize that the shot is more difficult to perform the farther you move away from the net. Learn to take a little speed off the shot and focus more on placement as you get farther from the net.

Letting the ball bounce before attempting the smash is often a wise move, especially if the lob is extremely high or is headed for the backcourt. Allowing a ball to bounce first normally results in a more consistent smash because the ball spin has been eliminated and more time is available for getting your body into correct hitting position. You should practice the smash drill with a bounce as much as without a bounce. Start 5 to 7 feet away from the net and work your way back to the baseline.

General Comments. Good timing is vital toward success in hitting the smash, with correct body positioning being equally important. Learn when to let the ball bounce and when to take it out of the air. Such factors as ball height, location and the actual game situation should be considered, along with your ability to successfully hit a smash.

LOB DRILLS

Bounce and Lob Drill

Objective. To develop the proper stroke mechanics for the lob shot.

Description. The lob shot can be either a defensive or offensive shot, depending on the position of your opponent and the actual game situation. Both types should be practiced. An offensive lob is 12 to 15 feet high, a height that allows the ball to pass over an opponent's maximally extended racket, even when he/she jumps to hit the ball. This shot is called an offensive lob because the opponent does not have time to retreat backward and return the ball. A defensive lob is a much higher shot that can also be a difficult shot to return. However, it permits enough time for a player to reposition him/herself and make the return. All lob shots should be hit deep in the backcourt and are more effective when hit to the opponent's backhand side.

Stand in the center of the court at the service line while facing the net, and bounce a ball to your forehand side. As you did in the ground stroke positioning drill, step into the ball (pivot, step, swing and follow-through) and hit a forehand lob. The swinging motion for a lob is an underhand low to high motion. Focus first on ball height and placement by attempting to keep the lob deep in the backcourt. Later, hit the lob deep to your imaginary opponent's backhand side.

Next, practice the lob with your backhand, because the development of this shot is necessary for playing highly competitive tennis. As you develop consistency, move away from the net until you are lobbing from beyond the baseline. Your progress may be accelerated if your partner stands at the net on the opposite side. He/she should stand about 5 feet from the net with a racket held high into the air. This enables a player to better estimate the desired height of both the offensive and defensive lobs.

General Comments. Although an intermediate or advanced stroke, the lob shot is an important part of any tennis game at those levels. Involving a slower than normal swinging motion, the shot is a rather difficult one to hit with accuracy. Be patient and concentrate on the hand-eye coordination and follow-through associated with the shot. Do not let the slower swinging motion allow you to think the lob is an easy shot. The lob in particular requires a lot of practice to develop.

Partner Lob and Return Drill

Objective. To improve the lob shot while concentrating on the correct positioning and body movement.

Description. Two players stand on opposite sides of the court at the baseline and face the net. One player starts the drill by hitting a ground stroke into the opponent's backcourt and moving forward toward the net. The other player returns the ground stroke with a lob shot while paying close attention to correct body positioning and ball height. Work on forehand lobs before trying any practice trials on the backhand side. By having one player at the net, a game situation is simulated. The player at the net can concentrate on the overhead smash shot, which allows both players to benefit from the drill. The shot sequence is a ground stroke, lob and smash. The partners should reverse roles periodically so each can practice both the lob and smash.

General Comments. The player who starts the drill with a ground stroke should not rush the net until the partner has had ample opportunity to practice both a forehand and backhand lob. This gives the player executing the lob shot a little more time to build confidence. This drill may be started with a serve instead of a ground stroke, in which case the shot sequence is a serve, lob and smash.

As you improve your basic skill in hitting the lob shot, concentrate more on deep court placement to the backhand side and vary the height of the lob. Also, make a habit of returning to the middle backcourt position after every shot during your drill work. This habit will make you a more fundamentally sound and competitive player.

DROP SHOT

Bounce and Drop Shot Drill

Objective. To practice the stroke technique of the drop shot.

Description. Stand in the middle of the court and face the net while standing about 10 to 12 feet away. Bounce a ball to your forehand side and hit a drop shot over the net. Think about the rather unusual swing that is associated with the shot. To hit a good drop shot, the swing should be a downward "chop" or up-to-down motion. The ball possesses underspin or backspin when leaving the racket. The backspin causes the ball to "bite" or bounce back toward the net and away from the opponent. Although the majority of drop shots are hit from the forehand side, you might want to practice a few backhand drop shots in case the game conditions dictate the need to attempt the shot.

Move toward the service line while performing the shot as your skill increases. The ideal drop shot barely clears the top of the net and hits in the front part of the forecourt. The swinging motion is a deliberate, slower-paced swing that emphasizes spin and placement. The angle drop shot is normally preferred and should be directed to the opponent's backhand side more often than to the forehand.

General Comments. The drop shot is a difficult shot to properly and consistently execute, even for advanced players. It is a "finesse" shot that leaves very little room for error. The swing has to be near-perfect in both speed and timing. Strategically speaking, the shot is a good one to have control of, since a well-placed drop shot is an extremely difficult shot to reach, much less to return. The shot is often used when a player is hitting from the service line or closer to the net and the opponent is in a baseline position.

Partner Drop Shot and Return Drill

Objective. To improve performance on the drop shot while concentrating on correct court positioning and body movement.

Description. Stand behind the service line in the center of the court while facing the net. Have your partner hit controlled ground strokes from the baseline to your forehand side for you to return with a drop shot. Initially, concentrate on moving toward the ball and getting into proper position for hitting the ball with the up-to-down or chop swing motion. Eventually, emphasize ball placement and spin. Continue to work on angle drop shots while gradually increasing the speed of your swing and imparting more backspin to the ball.

A drop shot from the baseline is a difficult, low percentage shot, but it might be a good idea to spend some time practicing the shot. This forces you to concentrate more and helps you to realize that the most effective drop shot is normally hit from the service line or closer.

General Comments. Practicing a backhand drop shot should be considered an optional drill, depending on your skill level. In the partner drop shot drill, one player should practice the drop shot return. In your attempt to make this difficult return, try to hit the ball to the backcourt if possible. Players who try to do too much with this return lose too many unnecessary points in a real game. Remember that excessive spin on the drop shot and the resulting unusual bounce the ball takes are two contributing factors in making the drop shot return a difficult stroke, in addition to the fact that the ball must usually be hit while the player is moving rapidly forward.

HALF VOLLEY SHOT

Half Volley Return Drill

Objective. To learn the correct hitting technique for the half volley shot.

Description. The half volley is not a planned shot, yet it is sometimes necessary and therefore should be practiced. When a player hits a half volley shot, it means that he/she is either out of position or has no other choice due to the opponent's good placement.

Stand facing the net while at the service line and in the center of the court. Your partner should hit ground strokes from the baseline in such a manner that the ball bounces directly in front of or on the service line. In other words, the ball should bounce at your feet. The swinging motion is similar to that for a ground stroke except that a quicker, snappier swing is required because a player normally does not have time to complete a full swing. Ball contact should occur immediately after the ball hits the playing surface or early during its upward flight. Solid contact should be made to consistently get the ball back over the net. After you have developed the basic hitting technique, work on keeping the return deep and to your opponent's backhand. Hit forehand half volleys first and then go to the backhand.

General Comments. Due to the difficulty of hitting the half volley, avoid the tendency to try to execute a tricky return. Just make sure the ball gets over the net, preferably deep to your opponent's backhand but at least over the net. Pay particular attention to the position of your racket head when the ball makes contact. Your racket head should be almost perpendicular to the playing surface; otherwise the ball tends to "fly" off the racket over the opponent's baseline.

FOOTWORK DRILLS

Footwork and proper body positioning are very important elements in the game of tennis. The ability to properly execute all the previously discussed tennis strokes does not mean a thing if you cannot get to the ball. Shot anticipation is an important variable related to proper body movement and positioning, but there is no drill available for practicing this component. The following footwork drills have been selected for their practicality in relation to an actual tennis game. You should spend 10 to 15 minutes at the end of each practice session working on proper foot placement and general conditioning, both of which can be achieved through the following drills. Incidentally, you should hold a racket in your hand for all the footwork drills, but you do not need a tennis ball.

Ground Stroke Step Drill

From a ready position, pretend to bounce a ball to your right side, then step into the imaginary ball as if you were going to hit a forehand. Quickly get back to the ready position and do the same thing on the backhand side. After the completion of each alternating ground stroke, assume the ready position, and keep the footwork (pivot, step, swing and follow-through) going continuously for 60 seconds.

Ground Stroke Run Drill

Assume a ready position at the center mark of the baseline and imagine that a ball has been hit to your forehand side. Run to the right half of the service line and stroke an imaginary forehand, then quickly get back to the baseline in the ready position. Do the same thing on the backhand side, and continue to alternate sides continuously for 60 seconds.

Serve and Run Drill

Start with a service motion from the baseline, followed by a run to the net. Hit an imaginary volley shot at the net and quickly retreat to the baseline. Keep this sequence going continuously for 60 seconds.

Side-to-Side Drill

Face the net and assume a ready position at the center of the service line. Imagine that a hard ground stroke is hit to your forehand side. Run straight across the service line, and when you reach the alley, hit an imaginary forehand and quickly return to the original position. Next, pretend that a hard ground stroke is hit to your backhand, and return the shot as before. Continue this side-to-side movement for 60 seconds.

Run, Jog and Stroke Drill

Predetermine eight imaginary spots on the court from which you like to hit a ground stroke. Make sure your locations generally cover your half of the court. Number them one through eight, so you will be able to move through the eight locations in numerical order. Start from the baseline and run to the first spot, then proceed to jog in place for 10 seconds before hitting an imaginary ground stroke. Then run to the second spot and complete the same sequence (jog in place, stroke and run). Continue the drill until you have completed the sequence at the eighth spot.

IV

Planning and Implementing Singles Strategy

PERCENTAGE TENNIS

Percentage Tennis Concept

Every game situation in tennis offers a player the opportunity to employ certain shots or tactics that demonstrate good potential for success against his/her opponent. The performer that consistently plays the odds with high percentage maneuvers during a game is making use of a strategy known as "percentage tennis." Utilization of this strategy enables players of all ability levels to more rapidly play at maximum proficiency. This method of intelligent play is an effective means of neutralizing any weaknesses in a player's game.

Principles of Percentage Tennis

Several qualities characterize the percentage tennis player. Perhaps the most general trait is a disciplined court manner that tends to give the percentage player a psychological edge over the average opponent. This heady performer patiently probes at his/her opponent's weaknesses with reasonably safe shots until presented a good opportunity to exploit the opponent's weak or low percentage return. The opponent is put into a compromising position by having to return balls that the percentage player places deep in the backcourt, a common tactic in percentage tennis.

The more disciplined percentage player also has an advantage in concentration ability. Focusing close attention on ball movement while maintaining awareness of the opposing player's court position becomes a natural habit for the percentage tennis practitioner during competition. The tendency to hit balls over the lowest point of the net (middle), where the margin for error is greater, is another good habit of the thinking percentage player.

Proponents of the percentage game make a point to play within their ability. In other words, they capitalize on the strengths of their game and disguise their weaknesses by avoiding attempts at shots and other aspects of court play that they cannot perform proficiently, due to either limited experience or lack of ability. Keeping the ball in play dominates the percentage player's thoughts, for he/she is well aware that the player who makes the fewest errors in a game almost always wins. This does not mean that good shot execution is not a high priority in percentage play. Skill development in shot execution is just as important for the percentage player as it is for the more aggressive power player. However, the difference is that the more disciplined percentage performer resists the temptation to attempt shots that he/she cannot effectively execute.

Advocates of percentage tennis also recognize the importance of physical fitness by staying in proper playing condition. They know that the player slowest to tire possesses a distinct advantage in the deciding set of a match. Consequently, percentage tennis players try to methodically move opponents around the court through the employment of a diverse shot selection.

SERVICE IN SINGLES PLAY

Position of Server

A position of 3 feet or less from the center mark is recommended when serving on the right side. Serving from that location facilitates service to the receiver's backhand and promotes proper court coverage in defending against the opponent's return.

On the left side, a position about 3 to 5 feet from the center mark enhances success in serving to the receiver's backhand while also allowing the server good forehand position on service returns.

The developing player should habitually assume these service positions because this practice readily promotes consistency and skill in service placement. As a strategic maneuver, advanced players sometimes deviate from the above-recommended positions when serving. But the wisdom of this ploy could be questioned, as it violates an important principle of percentage tennis.

Pace and Placement of Serve

Service pace generally pertains to the velocity of the serve. You are advised to vary the service pace to avoid becoming predictable in type of serve.

Speed of the serve is determined not only by how hard the ball is struck but also by the amount of spin that is imparted to the ball. The hard flat serve gives the receiver less time to react but is more difficult to place in the opponent's service court than the slice or twist serve. Hitting to the outside of the ball produces a slice serve. The slice motion takes some speed off the ball and allows it to more easily clear the net than the flat serve. Slice serves from a right-handed server to a right-handed receiver angle toward the forehand side. Thus, placement of this serve to the receiver's backhand side causes the ball to bounce in his/her direction, forcing the execution of a rather difficult return. On the other hand, placing the slice serve to the forehand side forces the receiver wide of the service court to attempt the return. Again, this example refers to right-handed opponents. Slice serves should be placed deep in the service court for maximum effectiveness, but even shallow slices are effective if they possess excessive spin. The receiver must move to the far side of the court to retrieve them and thereby is not in good position to rush the net or return to the baseline.

Striking the ball to the inside with the racket constitutes a twist serve, which produces a reverse effect to the slice serve. In this situation, a right-hander's serve to the forehand side of a right-handed opponent tends to veer toward him/her, while the same serve to the backhand side forces the receiver to move laterally for the return.

Another type of pace that should be varied is the amount of time a server utilizes between serves. Sometimes the server can disrupt the rhythm of an opponent who is experiencing a "hot" streak by simply speeding up or slowing down the service routine. You are cautioned to not become unreasonable in your employment of this tactic.

Successful servers also demonstrate variety in service placement. They may serve wide, deep or directly at the receiver, depending on the game situation and the opponent's strengths and weaknesses. The crafty server further directs about 85 percent of serves to the receiver's backhand side, since virtually all players hit the backhand stroke less competently than the forehand.

Wide serves are effective against the receiver who is positioned toward one side of the service court or sets up in an extreme position either behind or in front of the baseline. Another strategic use of the wide serve is against receivers who are adept at placing underspin on service returns.

Deep serves can be a two-edged sword. When placed inside the service court, their percentage rate for success is high. But the deep serve is difficult to execute due to the low margin for error. It is particularly effective on the second serve, when the receiver usually moves a few steps closer to the net.

Serves hit directly toward the receiver tend to cause some indecision by him/her in determining how the return will be made. This serve also tends to overwhelm the opponent who requires an unusual amount of time to complete his/her swing at the ball. In addition, receivers who show proficiency in hitting angle returns are foiled in their effort by this type of serve.

A bad habit of less accomplished tennis players is to overhit the first serve and underhit the second. This practice results in a low percentage service game. You should strive to get at least two thirds of your first serves in the service court. This can be accomplished by hitting the ball with medium spin and controlled force. The second serve should be hit a little slower, with more spin. It should be placed deep and to the receiver's weaker side, which in most cases is the backhand.

Variety in the service game may be forfeited to some extent when an opponent possesses a major weakness that can be easily exploited. In those situations, the type of serve that most effectively attacks the particular weakness should be disproportionately used.

Net Approach on Serve

Approaching the net on the serve is usually beyond the beginner's capability, and even for the more experienced performer, the tactic is primarily restricted to the first serve. As a result, net rushing on the second serve should only be attempted in situations where experience reveals that your opponent is incapable of effectively combating the tactic.

A basic principle to remember when moving to the net on the serve is to generally follow the serve's line of flight. By bisecting the court in preparation for the return, you place yourself in proper position for moving laterally in either direction. This fundamental of percentage tennis should be routinely followed.

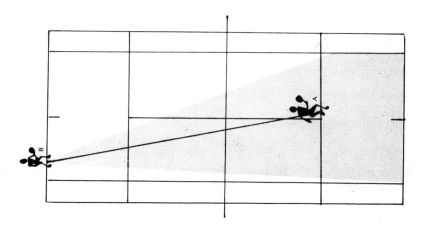

Fig. 92. Player A bisects player B's possible angle of service return.

You should decide beforehand when planning to rush the net on serve. After completing the serve, move quickly toward the net and come to a balanced stop at the moment your opponent contacts the return. Even on slower serves, you will not be able to escape "no-man's land," which means that your first volley of the opponent's return should be used as an approach shot for your net volley. Take a few more quick steps after you determine where the opponent's return is headed, then rapidly assume the hitting position for the first volley. Try to place the first volley deep, but avoid trying to overpower the ball.

When rushing the net in anticipation of the opponent's return of your first volley, try to locate an open area of the opponent's court to place your second volley. Unless an obvious opening exists, just try to place the ball deep in the opponent's court. This maneuver allows the opponent less angle for a passing shot, thereby often forcing him/her into hitting weak returns from his/her vulnerable position.

SERVICE RETURN IN SINGLES PLAY

The service return is not conducive to individual practice, so the only work most players get on this aspect of their game is during game play. This is one area of play whereby improvement will pay immediate dividends in your ability to break your rival's serve, the most obvious thing that you must accomplish to win a set or match.

Position of Receiver

The universally recommended position for awaiting serve is the "ready" position, shown previously in Figure 7. Either the Eastern forehand or Continental grip is appropriate for returning serve.

To choose an advantageous location for receiving serve, you must first determine where your opponent will stand in performing the serve. You should then assume the ready position at one end of an imaginary line between you and the server which bisects the resulting service court angle. This means that you have equal distance on the forehand and backhand sides to maneuver and attempt the service return. For hard serves, set up behind the baseline a couple of steps or so, and move in accordingly on slower serves. The second serve of some players is so slow and weak that the proper receiving location is several feet inside the court.

Experienced players sometimes assume an extreme position in the general service return area as a psychological ploy against the opponent. They may move up, back or to the side to disrupt the server's service concentration or to coax their opposition into serving a ball that provides them a good opportunity for a high percentage return. While the service toss is in the air, the receiver has time to assume a less extreme position. This tactic should not be used unless you demonstrate a reasonable degree of proficiency in returning serve.

For players with a weak backhand, it is a good idea to shade the backhand side somewhat to favor the forehand return. Even for the accomplished player, this is a sound practice, because the advantage of receiving more forehand return opportunities outweighs the disadvantage of relinquishing a small amount of service court space on the forehand side.

Service Return Strategy

Most players limit the power serve to the first attempt. Setting up deep to combat the power serve is the first step toward achieving effective results. One recommended way for controlling the return of a hard serve is to aim the ball back on line with the server. This return is particularly effective against servers who rush the net after serve, especially when the ball is hit low and hard. If an opponent's serve is too hard to control, try "blocking" the ball back with a half-swing motion. Much power is forfeited when the modified swing is used, but you are more assured of keeping the ball in play. When resorting to this type of return, try to hit the ball deep to your rival's backhand side.

Be aggressive on the opponent's second serve. Move in toward the net a suitable distance, and attempt a hard shot to the server's backhand. The hard, deep return will put you in excellent position to control the rally.

Players commonly apply more slice spin to the ball on second serves. A shallow receiving position promotes earlier ball contact, which neutralizes the effectiveness of the slice serve.

When playing someone who does not have a powerful serve, you can experiment more with power returns, especially with the forehand. Deep cross-court shots and down-the-line returns are good alternatives to the ball that is directed toward the server's feet. Shallow down-the-line returns are also effective shots when hit with great force.

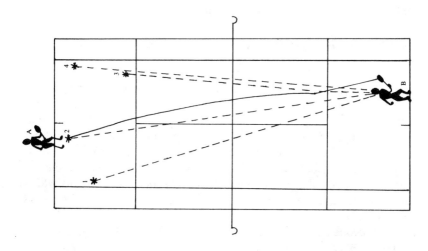

Fig. 93. Player B's power service return options on player A's weak serves: (1) deep cross-court return; (2) return at server's feet; (3) shallow down-the-line return; (4) deep down-the-line return.

A player who experiences difficulty in hitting backhand service returns can partially nullify that weakness by learning to chip the ball back with underspin. Although this type of return is less effective than one hit with power, it is a reasonably safe return when placed deep in the backcourt.

When returning serve against a baseline opponent, give him/her a steady diet of deep, medium-speed returns. The advantage that is generally conceded to the server will be negated.

Occasional lob returns to the opponent's backhand can prove fruitful against a net rusher. Moreover, drop shots should be used sparingly as service returns because of their low percentage effectiveness.

71

General Tips for Returning Serve

One tip that is high on the list of percentage tennis principles is to play the serve on the rise at the top of its bounce. This also holds true for hitting strokes during a rally. Fewer errors result from this practice, and the opponent has less time to set up for your return.

Show patience in the service return game by playing within your ability. Avoid unforced, low percentage return attempts. The resulting consistency in your return of serve will help to offset your weaknesses. When all else fails, just try to keep the ball in play. Since most points in tennis are won on errors, your opponent's mistakes may enable you to stay in the game.

In summary, remember that the basic plan for returning serve in percentage tennis is to vary the returns while probing for weaknesses in the opponent's game. Once these shortcomings surface, you should alter your service return approach accordingly. Stay with the percentage shots you execute best, particularly on crucial points.

CONTROLLING RALLY IN SINGLES PLAY

General Tips for Controlling Rally

In order to maximize your performance in singles play, you must apply the basic principles of percentage tennis. The two key objectives of the percentage game are to attack the opposing player's weaknesses and to avoid unnecessary errors on your side of the net. Tennis experts estimate that three of every four games played are won due to errors of the opposition, not because of the quality of offensive execution. Be determined to challenge your foe to perform beyond his/her ability while at the same time taking precautions to not become a victim of your own strategy.

The one percentage tennis principle that will take you the greatest distance in competition is the tactic of stroking the ball deep to the backcourt as often as possible. Balls placed near the baseline require an opponent to retreat backward in preparation for a shot that presents a much smaller margin for placement error than one taken inside the court. The player forcing his/her opponent deep is presented with a good opportunity to either approach the net and put away the opponent's return or advance to a desirable position for a high percentage approach shot that may lead to a winner on his/her next stroke opportunity. Forcing your rival to backpedal beyond the baseline to return a ball provides you much time to set up for his/her return, while the opponent is allowed little time to resume a proper court position for his/her next return.

Equally important as hitting the ball deep in the backcourt is the practice of returning to "home base" between strokes. Home base is a position about one step behind the baseline, generally behind the service mark, which is midway between the sides of the court. In anticipation of an opponent's return, this is the most advantageous position on the court for initiating movement to the ball and performing high percentage shots. Of course, the home base maneuver does not apply when a player wishes to rush the net for an approach or net shot, or in situations where he/she is forced to hit the ball from the area between the baseline and service line because of lack of time for returning to home base.

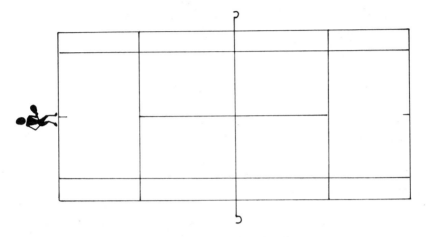

Fig. 94. Home base position.

The court space between the baseline and service line is called "no-man's land" and should be vacated as much as possible. When an opponent's return takes you into that area, and once your return is completed, the percentage move is to either rush the net if the opportunity is feasible or retreat back to home base if time permits.

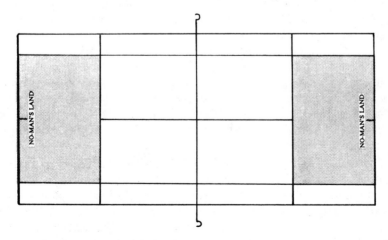

Fig. 95. "No-man's land," a slang term for backcourt.

Another percentage tennis principle that bears repeating is the practice of bisecting the possible angle of return by an opponent. This is a situation when the home base position or midcourt position at the net must be adjusted to some extent to ensure that proper court position is assumed in preparation for the opponent's return. In other words, the angle of the area within the boundaries of the defender's side of the singles court varies according to the offensive player's location when he/she hits the ball. By assuming a position in or near the middle of the angle, the player allows relatively equal distance on the forehand and backhand sides for responding to his/her opponent's return.

Percentage tennis players know that the ability to concentrate and play with patience takes on added significance at certain key points in a game. A disciplined style of play is most important on the crucial first and third points, and also when the score is 40–30, deuce or advantage.

Baseline Play

An astute blend of patience and aggressiveness is the key for success in baseline play. When hitting from the baseline, a deliberate, patient approach is recommended. Try to force your opponent into mistakes by consistently returning the ball deep in his/her court and by using a variety of shots to keep him/her off guard. Discipline yourself to attack the opponent's short returns. Contact the short balls on the rise, so your opposition will have less time to prepare for hitting your return.

Deep shot placement is the key for keeping a rival player away from the net. The deeper he/she has to retreat to return a ball, the more his/her return angle diminishes. Deep returns take longer to get back over the net, allowing the player on the other side of the court additional time to set up for his/her return. Do not overhit in your attempt to stroke the ball deep. Medium-speed returns can be effective shots, particularly those to your opponent's backhand side. A high bouncing ball to the backhand presents one of the most difficult shot challenges in tennis.

When playing a defensive type of player who prefers to play almost exclusively from the baseline area, keep in mind that he/she probably lacks confidence in hitting the volley and smash. Capitalize on these short-comings by occasionally luring him/her to the net with a well-placed drop shot. Remember to precede the drop shot with a shot placed deep in the backcourt. This will make your adversary's dreaded trip to the net even more discomforting.

Aggressive opponents will often get good position at the net despite your best efforts to keep them away. When this happens, try to hit your returns as low as possible without striking the net. Balls clearing the net by a narrow margin are difficult returns for the player who is either rushing the net or is already positioned there. In the case of the net rusher who has come to a balanced stop near the service line or beyond, returns directed at the player's feet force him/her to hit up on the ball, a practice that more often than not results in a weak return. The player at the net discovers that the low ball's close proximity to the net creates problems in picking up the ball's line of flight. The higher you hit the drive shot over the net, the lower your percentage for success becomes.

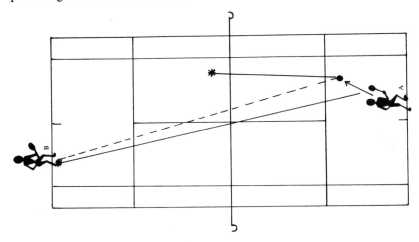

Fig. 96. Player A lures baseline player B to net with drop shot.

Use the whole court when hitting from the baseline. Cross-court passing shots are most appropriate against a baseline player. They clear the net at its lowest point and, in regard to depth, have a greater margin for error, as the court is 5 feet longer when measured diagonally from corner to corner. The cross-court return should be hit with topspin because the resulting speed of the ball reduces the time the opponent has to react properly to the shot. Consequently, he/she becomes vulnerable to a passing shot or lob directed to the opposite side.

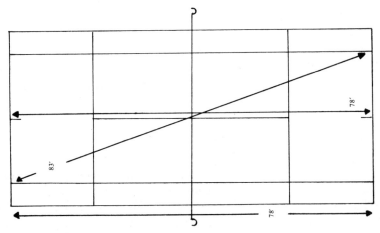

Fig. 97. Diagonal court is 5 feet longer than distance from corner to corner on same side or from center mark to center mark.

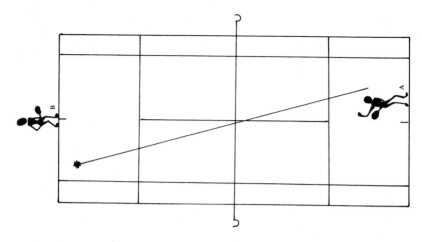

Fig. 98. Player A's cross-court passing shot clears net at its lowest point.

The down-the-line ball is the most common passing shot. Used against the net rush, it is hit with underspin, which promotes a higher arc as the ball passes over the net. This is necessary when hitting down a line because the net is higher on the sides, and the court distance is at minimum length.

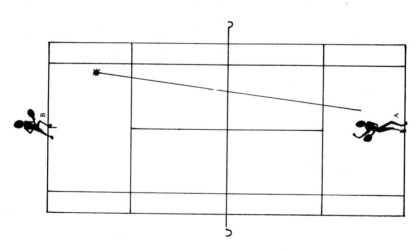

Fig. 99. Player A hits down-the-line passing shot.

Another effective shot against the player at the net is the lob. Most players underuse this valuable shot and frequently try to place it too close to the side line when they do. A placement just wide enough to make your foe hit the return with his/her backhand is sufficient. Use the lob with more discretion on windy days because the wind alters the flight of the lob more than any other shot in tennis.

Net Play

Beating an opponent to the net is a significant step toward victory in tennis. A higher percentage of winning shots are hit from the net position than anywhere else on the court. To begin the journey to the net, be alert for short balls hit by your opponent and capitalize on many of them. Balls landing at the service line and in toward the net fit into the short ball classification.

The approach shot should be hit down the line on the opponent's backhand side. Contact the ball on the rise in order to give the opposing player minimum time to respond to the approach shot. Remember that the down-the-line shot should be hit with underspin. With a series of short steps, follow the ball to the net and come to a balanced stop as the opponent contacts the ball. Break for a balanced position about an arm and racket's length from the net in line with the opponent's return. Sometimes the intended approach shot does not enable a player to reach the net. An intervening volley similar in placement to the preceding shot is the percentage shot in this situation. Again, take the net position described above.

On low opponent returns, volley the ball just over the net toward the open area of the court, and hit the high return hard and deep to that area. When having to perform the smash shot in response to an opponent's lob, remember to apply less power to the ball the farther you have to move from the net. The nearer the potential smash ball gets to the service line, the more you should consider letting it drop in favor of a forehand power stroke. Definitely forego the smash shot on balls landing beyond the service line.

V

Planning and Implementing Doubles Strategy

Teamwork and aggressive play are the essential ingredients for success in doubles tennis. The odds for winning are heavily in favor of the team that more readily controls offensive position at the net. This advantage is accomplished through adeptness in beating the opposing team to the net area and forcing the opposition into a defensive position in the backcourt. Superiority in net play is vital in doubles tennis because the attacking team is given the opportunity to hit forceful, high percentage returns. Even when successful in getting these difficult returns back over the net, the defending players must generally volley up on the ball, which plays into the strength of the awaiting team at the net.

While it is possible to play an effective baseline game in singles tennis, the chances for success in playing that type of game in doubles are extremely low. It is a low percentage game because pinpoint accuracy is required on passing shots and lobs. Many developing players avoid the fast-paced net game due to their inability to execute the required volley, smash and lob shots. If you are a beginner or intermediate performer who relies on a baseline game in doubles, you are advised to utilize the net game strategy in future doubles matches while also regularly practicing the volley, smash and lob strokes. By doing so, you will eventually reach your optimum potential in doubles, something you could never do by continuing to play the baseline game.

SERVICE IN DOUBLES PLAY

Position of Server and Partner

A strategic position for the server is about midway between the center mark and the side line. This allows the server relatively equal distance in each direction for covering his/her area of responsibility.

The recommended position for the server's partner during service is approximately 6 to 12 feet from the net and about 3 feet inside the singles line. Generally, the closer position is assumed on the first serve and on any type of serve that the receiver has experienced difficulty in returning effectively. More distance is allowed between the player's position and the net on the second serve and on weaker serves in general.

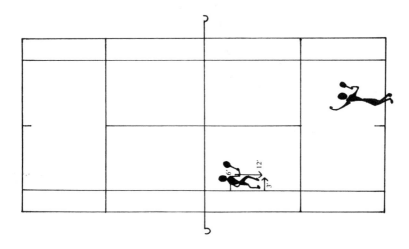

Fig. 100. Position of server and partner in doubles when serving to deuce court.

If a player stands roughly 3 feet inside the singles line, a proper coverage of the alley is assured. On wide serves in the ad court, it is sound practice to stand closer to the alley, while a position closer to the center of the court is advantageous in responding to a backhand service return from the deuce court.

Service Order, Pace and Placement

Since the player serving first in doubles actually serves more times than his/her partner in the set, it is common practice for the most effective server to initiate service for his/her team.

A worthy goal for the doubles server is to successfully place at least 75 percent of first serves in the opponent's service court. This is achieved by reducing the speed of the ball while increasing the amount of spin. Since flat serves are more difficult to place within the service court, they should be used judiciously in the doubles game.

Even less speed and greater spin should be applied to the second serve. It should be hit with topspin and placed deep in the service court. Although the placement percentage is high for the slower second serve, you should avoid serving the ball so slow that it sets up the receiver for high percentage returns.

For best results, vary the pace, spin and placement of the serve. Altering the speed of the serve can hinder the receiver's timing in hitting the returns. Mixing slice and twist serves and the amount of their break keeps the receiver guessing as to the type of serve that is coming. Furthermore, a certain number of serves should be placed wide to the receiver's side, while others are either directed toward any open area allowed or are hit directly at the receiver.

Serves to the backhand are always good percentage serves. They provide an opportunity for the server's partner to move to the net and cut off returns, particularly on serves to the deuce court. Deep serves to the receiver's backhand also give the server a good opportunity to rush the net. A twist serve to a right-handed player's backhand is effective because the spin imparted to the ball causes it to bounce in a diagonal direction away from the receiver.

Slice serves to the receiver's forehand in the deuce court tend to force him/her to the side of the court, which prevents the possibility of an effective net rush. A baseline doubles team is vulnerable to this serve because of the opening that it frequently creates in the middle of the court. Serving to the forehand in the ad court is a sound change-of-pace tactic. This serve can also be successful against the player who overplays the backhand side or has a tendency to overswing on the forehand.

Net Play on Serve

Getting to the net as quickly as possible after a serve should be a goal of every doubles server. The spin serves that are synonymous with the doubles game are major contributors to the server's ability to reach the net area in planned fashion. In singles play, the commonly used flat serve allows a server only a few steps before he/she must come to a balanced stop in anticipation of the opponent's return. The slower serves in doubles enable the server to often reach the vicinity of the service line, an advantage position for a successful volley and net rush.

To succeed in the net game on service, the server's partner must be adept at "poaching," the act of intercepting returns that are directed toward the server's side of the court. Used primarily on the first serve, the poach should be a planned aspect of the serving team's strategy. Experienced players routinely use some type of signal to the server when they are intending to poach. The signal can be a casual gesture that is difficult to detect, or the server's partner may choose to use the non-racket hand to relay some type of behind-the-back sign just prior to the service.

The poacher should take advantage of poor service returns by hitting hard volleys either low and wide of the opponent near the service line, at his/her feet, or between the opponents down the middle of the court. The poaching player's momentum often takes him/her into the server's side of the court. In those situations, it is a good idea for them to switch sides of the court in preparation for the next return.

Poaching is effective when strategically used. The practice demonstrates value on deep serves and in response to slow, underspin returns.

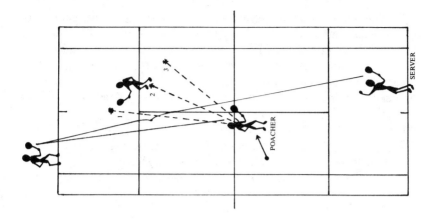

Fig. 101. Three effective shot options for poacher on service return: (1) return down middle of court; (2) return toward feet of player closest to net; (3) low and wide return.

Furthermore, it often disrupts the rhythm of the person returning serve, providing an added advantage for the service team. Teams that repeatedly use the poach try to place a higher than normal percentage of serves near the center of the court because most returns of this type of serve tend to be hit toward the middle of the court. More aggressive teams like to use the ploy on crucial points such as ad out.

Just as poaching is a bad habit on the second serve, it is generally poor strategy for the server to rush the net on that serve. When you sense that approaching the net would be risky, play patiently until a legitimate opportunity occurs. If your opponent chooses to stay at the baseline after returning serve, try to keep him/her back with deep returns. When he/she makes a break toward the net, attempt to hit the ball at his/her feet. Deep, low returns away from the net player are particularly high percentage shots in this situation.

SERVICE RETURN IN DOUBLES PLAY

Position of Receivers

Doubles receivers are best positioned when the player with the superior forehand plays the deuce court and the one having the stronger backhand is responsible for the ad side. When the same player possesses these strengths, the team must decide whether the better all-around player will receive in deuce court, where more receiving opportunities are presented, or in the ad court, where so many high-pressure returns must be skillfully executed with the game hanging in the balance. Further decisions have to be made when a left-handed player is a part of the receiving team. In this situation, the pros and cons of each order for receiving service should be justly considered before making a final decision.

The receiver normally assumes a ready position near the center of the service angle and in close proximity to the baseline and singles side line. Moving in from that position has advantages over the opposite alternative. A closer receiving position allows the player to hit a rising ball, a distinct advantage in returning serve. The margin for error in net clearance is greater for the receiver, and the opponents have less time to respond to his/her return. However, avoid moving in too far, or your supposed advantage will turn from an asset to a liability.

Receiving serve from a position beyond the normal location makes the player extremely vulnerable to wide serves of all types. However, you may sometimes be forced to retreat to a deeper location because you are unable to successfully deal with an opponent's powerful flat serve at your normal receiving position.

The position of the receiver's partner depends on the strength of the receiver's return. A safe position on most first serves is a few steps back of the service line and very near the service line on the second. The stronger the service return, the closer a player should be stationed to an area about 10 feet from the net, a position conducive to successful poaching. On the other hand, the recommended distance for retreating on weaker service returns extends back to an area just inside the baseline. It is also wise to move somewhat closer to the center of the court on weak service returns to protect against the inevitable down-the-middle returns. The receiver's teammate must give some ground to a successful poacher to properly cover his/her side of the court. The same is true in matches where the opponent server is consistently beating the receiver to the net.

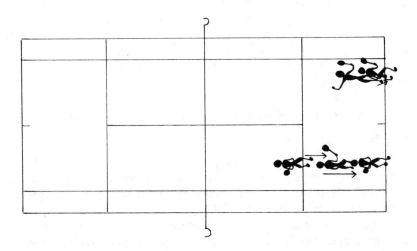

Fig. 102. Doubles receiving position varies according to effectiveness of opponent's serve.

Low service returns at a rushing server's feet provide a good opportunity for the receiver's partner to intercept the return at the net and hit a potential winner. The receiver's partner should definitely poach on low service returns toward the middle of the court.

Service Return Strategy

Breaking serve contributes to successful doubles tennis as much as winning serve does, but tennis literature commonly devotes more space to service technique and strategy. One possible reason why the service return phase of the games receives less emphasis than the serve does is that the former game component does not lend itself well to practice drill. Whatever the reason, the important thing is that at least one service break is necessary to win a set in doubles or singles tennis, and the service return is a major factor in the vast majority of service breaks.

The receiver has three basic shot options on the service return in doubles. The cross-court return, chip lob and down-the-line ball are all appropriate service returns in certain game situations. The cross-court shot is the highest percentage return when the ball is driven low and at the feet of the rushing server. This placement forces him/her to hit up on the return, a low percentage counter. The low shot also can be inhibiting to the server who likes to rush the net. The cross-court return that evades the server's reach can be a deadly return, but above-average placement skill is required. When the server's partner plays too close to the alley, an opening results that allows for a high percentage cross-court return that is directed more toward the middle of the court.

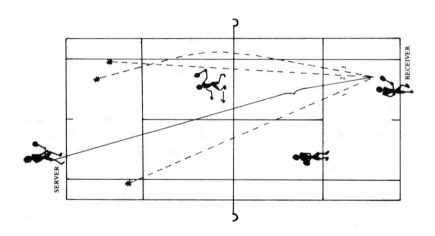

Fig. 103. Three effective service return options for doubles receiver: (1) cross-court return; (2) down-the-line return; (3) chip lob.

The chip lob hit to the backhand side of a net poacher can be effective, especially on serves from the deuce court. The reason is that most servers are right-handed and therefore must hit a backhand return because the chip lob requires them to move to the other side of the court to retrieve the ball. Generally, a lob return of serve is not recommended, but the poacher is restricted in his/her ability to recover from his/her precarious position to return the chip lob. Second, the chip lob has less arc than the regular lob, which means that the server has little time to cover the unusually long distance and return the ball.

The net player who tends to poach too early is vulnerable to the down-the-line service return. It is impossible for the overcommitted poacher to defend this shot when it is placed well.

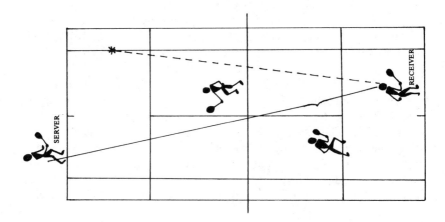

Fig. 104. Down-the-line return on early poacher.

In concluding this section, a general rule of thumb for returning service is worth mentioning. The principle is to drive the ball from a deep position and shorten the swing accordingly when receiving serves closer in toward the net. This good habit will help ensure that you return serve to the best of your ability. Should the recommended service return game fail you, use the returns that you can execute most successfully until you obtain or regain more versatility in this important phase of tennis.

CONTROLLING RALLY IN DOUBLES PLAY

Backcourt Play

Successful doubles tennis teams try to limit their participation in backcourt play as much as possible. They have learned through experience that superior forecourt play is the key to winning in doubles. Despite the secondary importance of the backcourt game, proficiency in this component of team play is also necessary for success. The basic purposes of

84

backcourt play are to defend that area of the court when necessary and to initiate the desired move to the forecourt with a timely, well-placed return. Thus, the backcourt game in doubles is viewed as a temporary method of play for meeting these purposes.

The passing shot is an integral part of the backcourt game. This shot must be hit low and hard for maximum effectiveness, and it derives best results when hit down the middle of the court. These type of returns often cause some indecision in the members of the opposing team as to who will return the shot, and they cross the net in the area of its lowest point. Wide passing shots can also be effective but are lower percentage returns.

Low soft shots from the backcourt force the opponents to hit up on the ball, often resulting in a short ball that presents a high percentage passing shot opportunity. Lob placement is also paramount from the backcourt position. Deep lobs are more effective, but short lobs are valuable for forcing the opposition into a defensive position in the backcourt.

When driven wide to make a return, remember that a shot down the line demonstrates a greater chance for success than one cross-court. The cross-court shot in this situation allows the forecourt opponents too much time to intercept the ball near the net and hit a high percentage return.

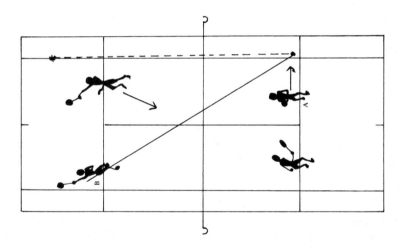

Fig. 105. Player A's down-the-line shot on player B's wide return.

Forecourt Play

To successfully apply percentage tennis principles in the forecourt, you must be able to hit the volley, lob and smash shots with proficiency. These are the key ingredients in the formula for obtaining maximum effectiveness in the doubles game. To further illustrate this point, experts contend that 75 to 80 percent of points are scored from the forecourt and that the vast majority of the forecourt winners are volleys.

When playing in the forecourt during a rally, one type of strategy is required for effectiveness against an opposing team in the backcourt and another is in order when the opponents are in the forecourt. Longer rallies tend to result when one team is stationed in the backcourt. The forecourt team must be patient and wait for an opponent's mistake that can be easily exploited. Short-angled volleys are effective for drawing the opponents in toward the net and forcing them to hit up on the ball, creating a scoring possibility for the team in the forecourt.

If all four players are at the net, each team is attempting to make the other execute a return that requires hitting up on the ball. The rising ball that results should be driven down the middle of the court, which requires a split-second decision by the opposition as to which player will attempt the return. Repeated drives down the middle of the court have another strategic value. They tend to draw the opposing players more toward the middle of the court, opening up ample court space between them and the side lines for high percentage returns.

Be prepared for a lob shot from your opponents at any time when playing in the forecourt. A rule of thumb is to position yourself at least 6 feet from the net when anticipating opponent returns. Otherwise, the lob is almost impossible to defend. Back up your partner on lob shots over his/her head if possible. Defense the lob with either a smash shot or another defensive lob, allowing the circumstances to dictate which choice is made. Short lobs that would fall in the forecourt if allowed to drop should be countered with a smash shot directed down the middle of the court or to an open area that may result on the shot exchange. The farther a lob drifts toward the service line, the less power should be used in hitting the overhead shot. In these situations, placement supersedes power in importance.

Lobs toward the service line area and beyond should be allowed to drop and then be combated with another lob or some other type of deep return.

General Tips for Controlling Doubles Rally

Many general principles of strategy for rally play in doubles are worthy of mention. Balls down the middle of the court should be returned by the player in the forehand position, with exceptions made in situations where a player has a stronger backhand volley. Short balls are more effectively returned by the player closer to the net. When these balls require a player to move into his/her partner's side of the court, the pair must quickly switch court positions until the rally is terminated or another legitimate switch becomes necessary.

When preparing for a net rush, return the ball low to the feet of the deeper player. On high returns, the net player should hit the ball toward the feet of the closer player. In each situation, the opponent is forced to hit up on the ball.

A player should cover the middle of the court when his/her partner is forced into the doubles alley or off the court to return a shot. When you are forced wide to hit a ball, remember that a shot down that particular side line is the best percentage return.

Another principle of strategy in doubles tennis is to counter a drop shot with another drop shot. This tactic forces one of the opponents to charge the net for a reasonably difficult return. Your favorable net position will allow you to exploit the high and sometimes soft returns that frequently result when a player is forced to hit up on the ball.

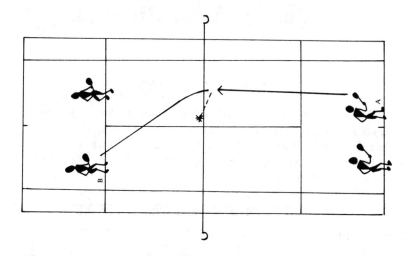

Fig. 106. Player A counters player B's drop shot with another drop shot.

VI

Evaluating Your Progress

SKILLS TESTING

The two skills tests presented in this chapter are designed to measure a player's general tennis ability. Test items for measuring skill in the service, forehand and backhand strokes are included, as well as an item for assessing rally ability. The value of these test items as indicators of general tennis ability was substantiated in research studies by the test developers.

HEWITT TENNIS ACHIEVEMENT TEST

Description

The purpose of this test is to measure achievement in the basic tennis skills of the service, forehand and backhand drives. Specific test items include the forehand drive placement, backhand drive placement, service placement and speed of service. The court markings for the test items are shown in Figures 107 and 108. In each of the tests, a ¼ inch rope is stretched above the net at a height of 7 feet.

Educational Application. The test is designed for college men and women of all ability levels, including varsity performers. Furthermore, it is useful for measuring tennis achievement of high-school boys and girls at the aforementioned levels.

Administrative Feasibility

Time. Accessibility to three courts would promote the test's administration in one 60-minute class period for a class of 15 to 20 students.

Personnel. An instructor should serve as scorer for the service placement and speed of service test items, while trained assistants are utilized wherever deemed necessary.

Training Involved. A student in the advanced group should have completed at least one academic term of tennis instruction or its equivalent as determined by the instructor.

Prior to testing, each subject is given ten minutes of practice time on the three skills to be measured. The forehand and backhand drive test is immediately preceded by five practice strokes.

Equipment and Supplies. Necessary items include a box or basket to serve as a ball container, three dozen new heavy-duty tennis balls and a variety of tennis rackets. Scoring materials and equipment for applying the court markings are also needed. Two poles, ladders or some suitable alternative are required to hold the rope taut in the service placement test.

Facilities and Space. At least two regulation tennis courts should be available to allow testing to be conducted on each court simultaneously.

Directions

Service Placement. The subject serves ten balls into the service courts as shown in Figure 107. The ball must be served between the net and the rope to be scored. Balls hitting the net are repeated.

Speed of Service. Ten good serve placements are scored according to the distance each serve bounces. This test item may be scored at the same time the service placement item is scored.

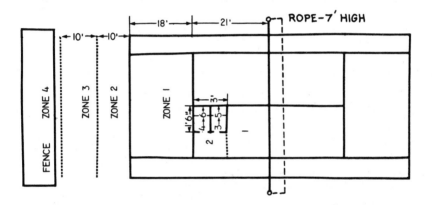

Fig. 107. Court markings for service placement and speed of service tests. From J. E. Hewitt, "Hewitt's Tennis Achievement Test," *Research Quarterly, 37:* 231–240, 1966. Reprinted by permission of AAHPERD.

Forehand and Backhand Drives. The subject takes a position at the center mark of the baseline. The instructor is stationed with a box or basket of balls on the other side of the net at the intersection of the center line and the service line. The instructor hits the five practice strokes to the subject prior to the ten test trials that are given for both the forehand and backhand strokes. The student chooses which ten balls to hit with the forehand and backhand.

The student should attempt to hit the ball under the rope to maximize his/her scoring potential. The same instructor should hit to all students for the purpose of test standardization. Net balls are repeated.

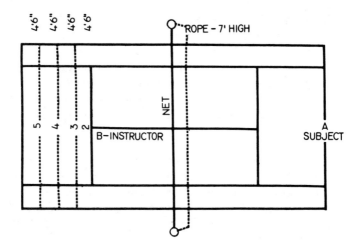

Fig. 108. Court markings for forehand and backhand drive test. From J. E. Hewitt, "Hewitt's Tennis Achievement Test," *Research Quarterly, 37:* 231–240, 1966. Reprinted by permission of AAHPERD.

Scoring Method and Norms

Service Placement. The point value for the zone in which each ball lands is totaled for the ten trials and is recorded as the official score. Balls served long, wide and over the restraining line (rope) receive a zero score.

Speed of Service. For each of the ten service placements that are scored, the appropriate speed of service score is assigned according to the zone values shown in Figure 107.

Forehand and Backhand Drives. Drives that clear the net and go under the restraining rope are assigned point values in relation to where they land in the court. Balls that hit over the restraining rope and land in a scoring zone receive one-half the regular values. Balls that are wide or long receive a zero score.

HEWITT TENNIS ACHIEVEMENT SCALES

Grade	Service Placements	Service Speed	Forehand Placements	Backhand Placements
	Junior Varsity and Varsity Tennis (16 subjects)			
F	20–24	20–22	25–28	20–23
D	25–29	23–25	29–32	24–27
C	30–39	26–32	33–39	28–34
B	40–45	33–36	40–45	35–40
A	46–50	37–40	46–50	41–47

	Advanced Tennis (36 subjects)			
F	11–14	8–10	24–25	22–26
D	15–19	11–13	26–29	27–30
C	20–30	14–21	30–39	31–37
B	31–37	22–25	40–44	38–42
A	38–44	26–30	45–48	43–46
	Beginning Tennis (91 subjects)			
F	1– 2	1– 3	1– 3	1– 2
D	3– 6	4– 7	4– 8	3– 7
C	7–16	8–13	9–21	8–19
B	17–21	14–17	22–28	20–26
A	22–26	18–21	29–36	27–34

From J. E. Hewitt, "Hewitt's tennis achievement test," *Research Quarterly, 37:* 231–240, 1966. Reprinted by permission of AAHPERD.

Additional Comments

The forehand and backhand drive tests could be improved with the use of a ball-throwing machine because the ball's speed and bounce would be more consistent than when hit by an instructor. The Hewitt Tennis Achievement Test is fairly comprehensive in measurement of overall tennis ability and lends itself to mass testing if appropriate facilities and personnel are available.

An interesting contribution of this test to tennis skills testing is its confirmation of the assumption that the bounce distance of a served ball is a valid indicator of its speed. This discovery greatly simplifies the test for speed of service.

KEMP-VINCENT RALLY TEST*

The purpose of this test is to measure achievement in tennis skill and to classify students by rally ability. Rally ability is determined according to student performance in a simulated tennis game.

Educational Application. The test is designed for college men and women but is also appropriate for secondary-school boys and girls.

Administrative Feasibility

Time. Two students can be tested every three minutes, which means the test is very feasible in time of administration.

Personnel. Three scorers are recommended, one to count the total hits of each subject and the other two to score the errors. The instructor

*From J. Kemp and M. F. Vincent, "Kemp-Vincent Rally Test of tennis skill, "*Research Quarterly, 39:* 1000–1004, 1968.

would probably be the logical choice to serve as the scorer assigned to count total hits.

Training Involved. One practice trial per subject in an earlier class period and a one-minute warm-up immediately prior to testing are recommended.

Equipment and Supplies. One stopwatch, four quality tennis balls per court and an assortment of rackets are required, along with scoring materials.

Facilities and Space. A regulation tennis court is all that is needed.

Directions

Two subjects assume opposing positions on a singles court. On the starting signal, one of the subjects bounces a ball from behind the baseline and puts it in play with a courtesy stroke. The students then proceed to keep the ball in play for three minutes. A ball hit into the net or out of bounds temporarily halts play until one of the subjects puts another ball into play. It is put into play in the same manner as was used to start the rally test. The use of any tennis stroke is permissible.

Four balls should be ready for use at the outset of the test. When these balls are used, the subjects must retrieve their own balls for the remainder of the test.

An error by a subject refers to (1) failure to put the ball in play with a courtesy stroke; (2) failure to hit the ball over the net in a rally; (3) failure to put a new ball in play from behind the baseline; (4) failure to keep the ball within the singles court area; and (5) failure to hit the ball before the second bounce.

As in singles tennis, balls hitting the boundary lines are in play, and those that strike the top of the net and land in bounds on the opponent's side are also playable. Balls landing out of bounds may be played at the discretion of the subjects for time-saving purposes.

Scoring Method

Initially, the total number of hits for the two students are counted, including those in which errors are committed. A courtesy stroke constitutes a hit. From the combined total hits of the two subjects, each subtracts his/her number of errors to determine the final rally score.

Additional Comments

The Kemp-Vincent Rally Test has a number of pluses not found in some of the other tennis skills tests. First, the test closely approximates game conditions, especially when the subject pairing is virtually equal. Second, the time involved in administering the test is relatively small for a test that measures general playing ability. Third, no special equipment or court markings are required, which contributes to ease of administration. Furthermore, the test eliminates the problem of inconsistency in force, direction and accuracy of balls thrown or hit to the test subject, as is common in other tests.

The test demonstrates one possible liability. A student capable of placing the ball so that it might easily be returned could contribute to an inflated score of the opponent and gross exaggeration of his/her true ability. However, the test truly has definite advantages over most of the other available tennis skills tests.

CHECKING YOUR KNOWLEDGE

A thorough understanding of stroke mechanics, rules, etiquette and strategy of tennis should be one of the goals for any developing player. Insight into these facets of the game will greatly complement the skill component of your game.

The following knowledge test is a teaching aid designed to help you increase your understanding of tennis. Questions on the test were derived from the information presented in this text. Completing the test before and after reading the book and then comparing scores is an interesting exercise you may wish to do. By the end of your tennis course, you should settle for nothing less than a 100 percent score on the test.

KNOWLEDGE TEST

True-False. Place **T** or **F** in blank at left. Answer is on page indicated.

_F_ 1. The modern game of tennis was introduced in France in 1873 (p. 3).

_T_ 2. Major T. H. Gem is given credit for introducing the game of tennis as we know it today (p. 3).

_T_ 3. The All England Club, now known as Wimbledon, was founded as a croquet club (p. 3).

_T_ 4. The former United States Lawn Tennis Association evolved into the present United States Tennis Association (p. 4).

_T_ 5. Tennis experienced a rapid growth in popularity in the 1970s (p. 4).

_T_ 6. USTA specifications for racket construction are very rigid (p. 4).

_T_ 7. Lightweight rackets are increasing in popularity (p. 5).

_T_ 8. Wooden rackets tend to be less expensive than those constructed of synthetic materials (p. 5).

_T_ 9. A player's hand size dictates the proper racket grip size (p. 6).

_T_ 10. Nylon racket string is recommended over gut for the majority of tennis players (p. 7).

_T_ 11. USTA guidelines for ball construction are specific (p. 8).

_T_ 12. The life span of a ball varies according to the court surface used (p. 8).

_F_ 13. A strict dress code for tournament tennis currently exists (p. 8).

_F_ 14. Clay courts or those of similar soft surfaces are the least common worldwide (p. 10).

_T_ 15. The height of tennis nets is greater on the ends than in the middle (p. 10).

_F_ 16. Clay courts require minimum maintenance (p. 10).

_T_ 17. Balls bounce more rapidly on synthetic court surfaces than on clay courts (p. 11).

_F_ 18. Grass is a popular court surface throughout the world (p. 11).

_F_ 19. The right service court is the same as the ad court (p. 12).

_F_ 20. Rules for doubles tennis vary greatly from the rules governing the singles game (p. 12).

_F_ 21. The term "deuce" properly describes a 30–30 score (p. 13).

_____ 22. Players are not required to switch ends of the court when the VASSS scoring system is employed (p. 16).

_____ 23. Matches generally require less time to play under the no-ad scoring system (p. 16).

_____ 24. It is proper etiquette for the server to call out the score before serving each point (p. 17).

_____ 25. The bulk of the hand is on top of the racket handle in the Eastern forehand grip (p. 21).

_____ 26. Use of the Continental grip is advantageous in doubles competition (p. 22).

_____ 27. High bouncing balls are difficult to hit when the Continental grip is utilized (p. 23).

_____ 28. Few tennis authorities advocate use of the Western grip (p. 23).

_____ 29. The Eastern grip promotes a more powerful stroke than the Continental grip when performing forehand shots (p. 23).

_____ 30. The ball toss on the serve should be released at about shoulder height (p. 25).

_____ 31. Racket-ball contact on the serve should be made at as high a point as possible (p. 25).

_____ 32. In performing the slice serve, the ball toss should be a little farther forward and more to the right than what is recommended for the flat serve (p. 26).

_____ 33. An early backswing contributes toward a successful forehand drive (p. 32).

_____ 34. The weight is on the forward foot at ball contact during the performance of a mechanically correct forehand drive (p. 33).

_____ 35. Topspin is produced on the ball by moving the racket head from high to low as the ball is hit (p. 33).

_____ 36. Balls hit with topspin rebound with greater velocity than do backspin balls (p. 37).

_____ 37. The traditional Eastern backhand grip is not recommended for use in performing the two-hand backhand (p. 22 & 37).

_____ 38. In terms of stroke mechanics, the overhead shot is very similar to the serve (p. 41).

_____ 39. The volley is considered to be a defensive shot (p. 46).

_____ 40. Little follow-through is required in the execution of a volley (p. 47).

_____ 41. Percentage tennis players show patience in their play and demonstrate concentration ability (p. 66).

_F_ 42. The recommended service position on the left side is closer to the center mark than it is on the right side (p. 67).

_F_ 43. Ball spin has no effect on ball velocity (p. 67).

_T_ 44. Hitting to the outside of the ball produces a slice serve (p. 67).

_T_ 45. Good strategy in serving includes the recommendation that about 85 percent of serves should be directed to the opponent's backhand side (p. 68).

_F_ 46. Wide serves have little value against receivers who place underspin on service returns (p. 68).

_F_ 47. Serves hit directly toward the receiver are considered to be poor serves (p. 68).

_T_ 48. Less skilled tennis players tend to overhit the second serve (p. 68).

_T_ 49. Rushing the net on the second serve is generally a bad practice (p. 69).

_T_ 50. Players tend to place more spin on the ball on second serves (p. 71).

_F_ 51. Drop shots are effective service returns (p. 71).

_F_ 52. In returning serve, the ball should be struck during its downward flight (p. 72).

_T_ 53. High bouncing balls to the backhand are difficult to return (p. 74).

_F_ 54. The cross-court ball is the most common passing shot (p. 76).

_F_ 55. Most players overuse the lob shot (p. 76).

_T_ 56. The lob shot is even more effective when playing outside on windy days (p. 76).

_T_ 57. A higher percentage of winning shots are hit from the net position than in any other area of the court (p. 77).

_F_ 58. Down-the-line returns should be hit with overspin (p. 77).

_F_ (59.) A smash is the proper shot selection in response to a lob shot directed beyond the service line (p. 77).

_F_ 60. Doubles play is more a baseline game than a net game (p. 78).

_F_ 61. A strategic position for the doubles server is as close to the center mark as possible (p. 78).

_F_ 62. Serving the first serve at maximum velocity is sound strategy in doubles play (p. 79).

_T_ 63. Slice serves are easier to place within the service court than the flat serve (p. 79).

96

64. Second serves should be hit with topspin and placed deep in the service court (p. 79).

65. Baseline doubles teams are vulnerable to the slice serve because of the opening it frequently creates in the middle of the court (p. 80).

66. Spin serves characterize the doubles game (p. 80).

67. The poach is most effective on the second serve (p. 80).

68. Receiving serve from an extremely deep position makes a player vulnerable to wide serves (p. 82).

69. Breaking serve contributes to successful doubles tennis as much as winning serve (p. 83).

70. The chip lob hit to the backhand side of a net poacher is an effective maneuver against serves from the deuce court (p. 84).

71. Regular lob shots have a greater arc than the chip lob (p. 84).

72. The vast majority of forecourt winners in doubles play are volleys (p. 85).

73. Forcing an opponent to hit up on the ball is a key principle of doubles strategy (p. 86).

74. The player closest to the net should play short returns in doubles (p. 86).

75. Countering a drop shot in doubles with another drop shot is sound strategy (p. 87).

Matching. Place proper letter in blank at left. Answer is on page indicated.

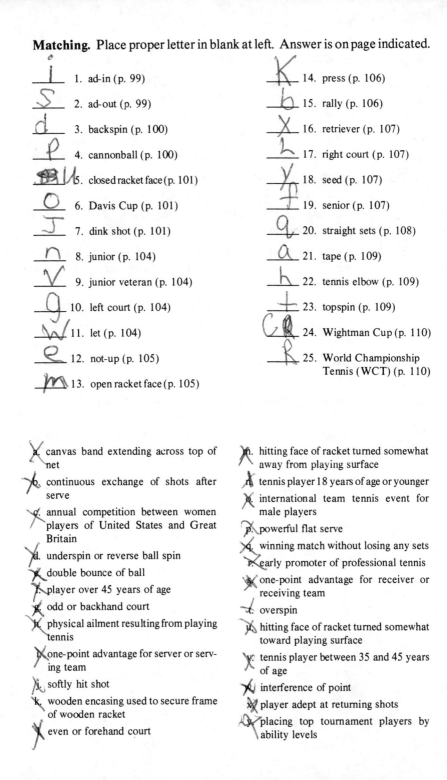

__i__ 1. ad-in (p. 99)

__s__ 2. ad-out (p. 99)

__d__ 3. backspin (p. 100)

__p__ 4. cannonball (p. 100)

____ 5. closed racket face (p. 101)

__o__ 6. Davis Cup (p. 101)

__j__ 7. dink shot (p. 101)

__n__ 8. junior (p. 104)

__v__ 9. junior veteran (p. 104)

__g__ 10. left court (p. 104)

__w__ 11. let (p. 104)

__e__ 12. not-up (p. 105)

__m__ 13. open racket face (p. 105)

__k__ 14. press (p. 106)

__b__ 15. rally (p. 106)

__x__ 16. retriever (p. 107)

__L__ 17. right court (p. 107)

__y__ 18. seed (p. 107)

__f__ 19. senior (p. 107)

__q__ 20. straight sets (p. 108)

__a__ 21. tape (p. 109)

__h__ 22. tennis elbow (p. 109)

__t__ 23. topspin (p. 109)

__c__ 24. Wightman Cup (p. 110)

__r__ 25. World Championship Tennis (WCT) (p. 110)

a. canvas band extending across top of net

b. continuous exchange of shots after serve

c. annual competition between women players of United States and Great Britain

d. underspin or reverse ball spin

e. double bounce of ball

f. player over 45 years of age

g. odd or backhand court

h. physical ailment resulting from playing tennis

i. one-point advantage for server or serving team

j. softly hit shot

k. wooden encasing used to secure frame of wooden racket

l. even or forehand court

m. hitting face of racket turned somewhat away from playing surface

n. tennis player 18 years of age or younger

o. international team tennis event for male players

p. powerful flat serve

q. winning match without losing any sets

r. early promoter of professional tennis

s. one-point advantage for receiver or receiving team

t. overspin

u. hitting face of racket turned somewhat toward playing surface

v. tennis player between 35 and 45 years of age

w. interference of point

x. player adept at returning shots

y. placing top tournament players by ability levels

Glossary
of Tennis Terms

Ace: Any serve an opponent or receiver is unable to touch with the racket; normally an exceptional serve from the standpoint of speed and placement.

Ad: An abbreviation for the word *advantage;* the first point scored after deuce.

Ad court: The left or odd service court from which all ad scores are served.

Ad-in: An abbreviation for *advantage in,* which means that an advantage of one point goes to the server or serving side after a deuce score.

Ad-out: An abbreviation for *advantage out,* which means that an advantage of one point goes to the receiver or receiving side after a deuce score.

All: An even or tied score, such as 15–15 or 30–30; verbalized as 15-all or 30-all.

All-court game: A style of play that successfully combines net play with baseline play.

All-court player: Refers to a player's ability to hit all tennis strokes competently, regardless of court position.

Alley: An area 4½ feet in width adjacent to the singles court that is a part of the playing court in doubles play after the serve.

Amateur: Any player who does not accept money for playing or teaching; plays for the enjoyment of the game and/or personal satisfaction.

American twist: An advanced serve that imparts both topspin and sidespin to the ball, causing it to take a high bounce in a diagonal direction from that in which it was originally traveling.

Angle shot: A ball returned at an extreme angle.

Approach shot: A ground stroke hit by a player who is advancing or will advance to the net; usually hit deep and to the opponent's backhand.

Association of Tennis Professionals (ATP): An organization comprised of male tennis professionals.

Australian doubles: A doubles formation in which the server and his/her partner at the net are on the same half or side of the court.

Backcourt: The playing area between the service line and the baseline.

Backhand: The stroke used to return balls that are hit on the left side of a right-handed player or on the right side of a left-handed player.

Backhand court: The left side of the court for a right-handed player and vice versa.

Backspin: A reverse or backward spin on the ball, causing it to rotate away from the direction of its flight. It is placed on the ball by a downward swinging motion of the racket called a chop or slice. Also referred to as *underspin*.

Backswing: The initial phase of a swing in which the racket is drawn back to prepare both the racket and the player's body for the forward swing.

Ball boy: An individual who retrieves balls for tennis players during competition, usually at the professional level.

Baseline: The end boundary lines of a tennis court, parallel to and 39 feet from the net.

Baseline game: A style of play or strategy that involves a player who consistently hits ground strokes from the baseline and seldom advances to the net.

Break point: The final point, if won by the receiver, that wins the game his/her opponent was serving. Also referred to as *break service* or *service break*.

Bye: A term commonly used in tournament competition that indicates a player does not have to play a particular round and automatically advances to the next round of the competition.

Cannonball: A powerful flat serve.

Carry: An illegal shot, which is carried on the racket strings, slung or hit twice.

Center mark: A line that divides the baseline into two equal halves; defines the service area as to the right and left sides.

Center service line: The line that is perpendicular to the net in the middle of the court and divides the two service courts.

Center strap: An anchor strap in the center of the net that allows for both net stability and an accurate net height.

Challenge round: The last round of a challenge-type tournament such as the Davis Cup competition.

Change of pace: A playing strategy whereby a player varies the speed of a return.

Chip: A modified slice, used primarily in doubles, which results in a short, angled shot.

Choke: Implies a bad or "blown" shot due to a very tense or high pressure playing situation.

Choke up: To use a higher than normal grip.

Chop: A stroke that requires a player to hit the ball with a downward and forward swing, thus imparting backspin to the ball.

Circular backswing: A backward, semicircular movement of the racket before initiating the forward swing.

Closed racket face: The angle of the racket's hitting face when it is turned somewhat toward the court or playing surface.

Closed stance: When both feet and the body are facing the side line; a side approach to the ball, which is used to hit most strokes.

Consolation: A tournament in which first round losers continue to play in the losers' bracket of the tournament.

Continental grip: A common tennis grip that involves a "V" shape created by the thumb and index finger. This grip can be used for the serve, forehand and backhand strokes; thus, a player does not have to constantly change grips.

Cross-court return: Any shot where the ball is hit from one side of the court across the net to the side diagonally opposite.

Davis Cup: An international team tennis event for male players with a predetermined format of four singles matches and one doubles match.

Dead ball: A ball that has lost air pressure and consequently does not bounce as it should.

Deep: Refers to a shot landing near the baseline in the backcourt. A deep serve, which lands in the service court near the service line.

Default: Failure to appear for a match or being unable to complete the match. The opponent automatically moves on to the next round.

Deuce: An even or tie score after six or more points of a game have been played.

Deuce court: The right half of the court; where a ball is served with a deuce score.

Dink: A softly hit shot, often with backspin, that just clears the top of the net and lands close to the net.

Double elimination: A tournament in which a player or team must lose two matches before being eliminated.

Double fault: Failure of the server to hit either the first or second serve into the proper service court. This results in a loss of one point for the server.

Doubles: A tennis match played with four people, two on each team. *Mixed doubles* refers to one male and one female player on each team.

Down-the-line return: A shot that is close to and parallel with the side line; often a high velocity shot that goes for a winner.

Draw: Players' names are written on a piece of paper and randomly drawn to determine their playing position and opponents.

Drive: An offensive ground stroke that is hit with power; often results in a point or is used as a defensive return.

Drop shot: Same as *dink shot.*

Drop volley: A drop shot that is hit before the ball bounces.

Earned point: A point that is won through skillful playing rather than as a result of an opponent's mistake.

Elimination: The termination of a player's tournament participation due to a loss or losses.

Eastern grip: A type of grip used to play the forehand and backhand returns.

Error: A point that is lost because of a player's mistake as opposed to one made by his/her opponent.

Even court: The right court, where an even number of total points have been completed for the particular game being played.

Face: The stringed hitting surface of the racket.

Fast court: A smooth-surfaced court that allows the ball to bounce low and rapidly toward the awaiting hitter.

Fault: A served ball that lands outside the proper service court; an illegal technique, position or return.

Federation Cup: International team competition for women with a predetermined format of two singles matches and one doubles match.

Fifteen: A term used in scoring that indicates the first point won by a player in each game.

Finals: The last round of a tournament, involving two players or teams competing for the championship.

Five: A slang abbreviation for fifteen; commonly used but is not an official term.

Flat drive: A shot hit in a straight line with very little arc or spin.

Flat face: Describes the position of a racket head when it is perpendicular to the court and facing the net; also called a *square face.*

Flat serve: A served ball that has little or no spin.

Floater: An undesirable shot, in which the ball has a high trajectory and is moving slowly across the net.

Follow-through: The phase of the swinging motion after the ball has been hit or contacted.

Foot fault: An illegal serve occurring when the server steps on or over the baseline before making contact with the ball.

Forcing shot: An offensive shot hit with exceptional power and good placement.

Forecourt: The playing area between the net and the service line.

Forehand: The stroke used to return a ball that is hit on the right side of a right-handed player or on the left side of a left-handed player.

Forehand court: The right side of the court for a right-handed player and vice versa.

Forfeit: Same as *default.*

Forty: A term used in scoring to indicate that a player has won three points in a game.

Forward swing: The forward motion of a racket before ball contact.

Frame: The part of a racket to which the strings are attached.

Game: Part of a set that is completed when one player or side wins four points while having at least a two-point lead, or wins two consecutive points after a deuce score.

Grand Prix: A combination round-robin and single elimination tournament for the top eight male point winners on the tennis circuit.

Grand Slam: When the same player wins all four major tennis tournaments: the championships of Australia, France and England (Wimbledon), and the United States Open.

Grip: The method or technique used for holding the racket handle; also refers to the material covering the handle.

Groove: The description of a tennis player's stroke pattern, leading to a smooth, consistent, disciplined return and a high degree of success.

Ground stroke: A forehand or backhand stroke used to hit a ball after it has bounced.

Gut: A type of racket string made from the intestines of an animal, such as a cat.

Hacker: A person who does not play tennis well; a player who has an unconventional style of play.

Half volley: A defensive stroke used to hit a ball immediately after it has bounced, with ball contact occurring below knee level. Technically speaking, it is actually a ground stroke and not a volley, since contact is made after the bounce.

Handle: The part of a racket that is gripped by the player's hand.

Head: The part of a racket, including the frame and strings, that is used to hit the ball.

Hold serve: Refers to a server winning a game.

In: A common, informal tennis term used for describing a shot that lands on the line or inside the playing area. A hand signal with the left hand held flat and the palm down signifies that a ball has landed inside the playing court.

International Tennis Federation (ITF): The organization that governs tennis throughout the world.

Invitational: A tournament open only to players who have been invited. Also referred to as a *closed tournament.*

Junior: A tennis player who is 18 years of age or younger.

Junior veteran: A tennis player between the ages of 35 and 45.

Kill: An offensive, winning shot that is hit with power and/or accuracy, such as a smash or drive.

Ladder: A tournament that places the competitors in a vertical column; by challenging and winning, a player may advance to the top or up the column.

Left court: Another name for the odd or backhand court.

Let: A serve that hits the top of the net and still lands in the proper service court. Also can indicate that a point was interrupted by interference, such as another ball coming into the playing area. In each situation, the point is replayed without penalty.

Linesperson: An official responsible for calling balls that land outside the boundaries of the court; most often used at the professional level.

Lob: A high, arching shot that passes over an opponent's maximum racket reach and lands near the baseline.

Lob volley: Same as a *lob,* except the ball is hit before it bounces.

Long: A common, informal tennis term indicating that a shot is hit out of bounds beyond the baseline. Holding a thumb high or pointing a finger is a hand signal that signifies that a long ball has been hit.

Loop: Refers to balls hit with topspin; the flight of the ball appears to dip sharply on its downward path.

Love: A term used in scoring to mean zero. In a love game, no points have been scored. In a love set, no games have been won by either player or team.

Match: A tennis contest between either singles or doubles players that consists of the best two of three sets to determine a winner. Male professionals often play the best three of five sets. Also used to refer to team competition between schools.

Match point: The final stage of a match, when a player or side that is ahead can win the match by winning one point.

Midcourt: The playing area near the service line or midway between the net and baseline.

Mixed doubles: A type of doubles competition in which each team consists of a male and female player.

Net: The material that is strung across the middle of a court and divides the court into two equal halves.

Net game: A style of play used by a player or team that frequently advances to the forecourt or close to the net after hitting a conventional ground stroke. This type of player or team hits many volley shots and smashes.

Net player: A player in doubles who plays near the net, or a singles player who frequently hits from the forecourt.

Net umpire: An official who is responsible for calling let serves; usually is found at the professional level.

No: Same as *long.*

No-ad: A form of scoring that eliminates deuce and the conventional love, 15, 30, 40 scoring system. The first player to attain four points (0, 1, 2, 3, 4) wins.

No-man's land: The midcourt area where balls often bounce at a player's feet, thus forcing a half volley return; area between service lines and baseline.

Not-up: A term that signifies a double bounce of a ball; a player failed to return a ball before the second bounce.

Odd court: The left court, where an odd number of total points have been completed for the particular game being played.

Offensive stroke: Any shot that is returned with the idea of either winning a point or forcing an opponent into an error.

On-the-rise: An aggressive style of play used by advanced players that involves hitting a ball before it reaches the height of its bounce. Because it is unconventional, it catches an opponent by surprise and allows him/her less time to react to the shot.

Opening: A high percentage scoring opportunity created by an opponent's mistake.

Open racket face: The angle of the hitting face of a racket when it is turned somewhat away from the court or playing surface; used to hit such shots as a lob, chop or slice.

Open stance: When both feet and the body are facing the net; a front approach to the ball.

Open tennis: Competition open to both amateur and professional players.

Out: Same as *long* or *wide.*

Overhead: A hard, powerful offensive stroke hit from an over-the-head racket position similar to a service motion.

Overspin: Spin imparted to a ball by hitting upward and through the ball. This forces the ball to spin in the same direction as its line of flight and causes a fast and high bounce.

Pace: The velocity with which the ball is hit; the amount of time a player takes between a point and the next service.

Passing shot: A ball that is returned out of the reach of an opponent; usually occurs when the opponent is positioned in the forecourt or at the net.

Percentage tennis: A strategy that promotes safe and somewhat conservative returns in order to reduce unnecessary errors. To hit the most effective shot for the particular game situation.

Placement: Ball control and shot accuracy.

Poach: A strategy in doubles whereby the net player leaves his/her normal position and moves across the court to intercept a volley shot that normally is returned by the net player's partner.

Point: The smallest scoring unit in tennis.

Point penalty: A method by which a player may be penalized points in a game for improper behavior.

Press: A wooden encasing used to secure the frame of a wooden racket to prevent possible warping.

Pro-set: A match that is completed when a player or team has won eight games and is ahead by at least two games.

Psyched-up: Describes a player exhibiting the emotional high that is often experienced before and during actual competition.

Pusher: A type of player who concentrates on control and consistency and hits with less ball velocity.

Put-away: A shot that is placed so well that the opponent has no chance of reaching the ball for a return attempt.

Qualifying round: A series of matches played before the actual start of a tournament to determine the players to be included in the playing field.

Quarterfinals: The round of a tournament in which eight players or teams remain in competition.

Racket: The instrument used in tennis to hit the ball.

Racket face: Same as *face*.

Racket head: Same as *head*.

Rally: A continuous exchange of shots between players after the serve; often incorrectly called a *volley*.

Ranking: The rating or listing of players based on such variables as the win-loss record, tournament results and opponents played.

Ready position: The proper court location and stance used by a player in preparation for returning a ball; normally a position in the middle of the court just back of the baseline.

Receiver: The player who is receiving the serve.

Referee: A tournament official who is responsible for supervising all phases of the particular competition.

Retrieve: The return of an opponent's shot; usually requires a long run or unusual effort.

Retriever: The type of player who is adept at getting the ball back over the net as a result of good speed and anticipation; however, this type of player lacks the ability or inclination to play an aggressive offensive game. Often referred to as a *hacker* or *pusher.*

Return: An unofficial term that means to hit a ball back to an opponent; often used to describe the return of a serve.

Right court: Another name for the *even* or *forehand court.*

Round: A designated level of tournament competition, such as first, second and third rounds. Half the remaining players or teams are elminated after the completion of each round; ultimately referred to as the *quarterfinals, semifinals* and *finals.*

Round-robin: A type of tournament in which every player or team plays all other players or teams. The winner is the player or team having the best overall record.

Rush-the-net: A style of play by which a player, after hitting an approach shot, advances to the net in preparation for a volley return.

Second: An unofficial term used to indicate that a player is ready to attempt the second serve.

Seed: To place the top tournament players by ability levels. Seeding is designed to prevent top players from competing against one another during the early rounds of the competition.

Semifinals: The next-to-last round of a tournament, in which four players or teams remain in the competition.

Senior: Any player over 45 years of age.

Serve: The stroke used to initially put the ball in play or to start either a game or point.

Server: The player who is serving.

Service: Applies to the served ball or the right to be the server.

Service break: Same as *break point.*

Service court: The area into which a ball must be served; located diagonally across the net from the server and bordered by the net, center line, service line and the singles side line.

Service line: The line that denotes the back of the service court, parallel to and 21 feet away from the net.

Set: A scoring unit of a match that has been completed with either a player or team having won six games with at least a two-game advantage. Should a tie-breaker not be used, play continues until a two-game lead has been attained after a 5–5 or 6–6 game score. In the case of a tie-breaker after a 6–6 game score, the set winner is determined by the particular tie-breaking system used, and the set score is recorded as 7–6.

Set point: The final point of a set if won by the player who is ahead in score.

Shaft: The part of a racket that is located between the handle and throat.

Side line: The boundary line that runs from the net to the baseline and marks the outside edge of the playing surface. The inside lines help enclose the boundaries for singles play, while the outside lines (4½ feet from inside lines) do the same for doubles tennis.

Sidespin: When a ball spins on its vertical axis and bounces to the side, as opposed to a straight, forward bounce.

Single elimination: A tournament whereby a player or team loses only one match before being eliminated.

Singles: A match played between two players.

Slice: To hit a ball with backspin; similar to a chop or chip shot.

Slice serve: To hit a served ball with sidespin, creating a higher than normal bounce to the side.

Slow court: A rough-surfaced court, which causes a ball to bounce high and slow.

Smash: Same as *overhead.*

Spin: Ball rotation caused by hitting a ball with the racket head at an angle, such as a chip, chop or slice shot. The three basic types of spin are topspin, sidespin and backspin.

Split: An unofficial expression that indicates two players or teams have each won one set.

Straight sets: To win a match without losing a set.

Strap: Same as *center strap.*

Stroke: The method by which a tennis ball is hit.

Sudden death: A method of breaking a tie score (6–6); normally referred to as the 5-of-9-point tie-breaker.

Sweet spot: The ideal hitting area on the strings; located in the center of the racket head. Balls hitting in this spot produce less racket vibration and better results.

Take two: An unofficial tennis expression that indicates to the server that the first serve may be repeated without penalty, for whatever reason. The receiver or server usually makes the decision unless tournament officials are in control of the match.

Tape: The canvas band extending across the top of the net.

Teaching pro: An individual who gives lessons or instructions for money, as compared to a playing professional who plays for money. Many individuals are both teaching and playing pros.

Tennis: A popular, competitive, lifetime-oriented game that can be played by two or four players. Derived from a French verb, *tenez,* which means to hold, take or receive. The implication is that a server must hold a ball and the attention of the receiver before starting a game.

Tennis elbow: A rather common neuromuscular condition of the elbow that results in pain and soreness and is thought to be caused by an improper hitting technique.

Thirty: A term used in scoring to indicate that a player or team has won two points.

Throat: The part of a racket between the handle and the head; inappropriately referred to as the *neck.*

Tie-breaker: A method of completing a set when the score is tied 6–6. Competing players may select either the 5-of-9 or 7-of-12-point tie-breaker.

Topspin: Same as *overspin.*

Trajectory: A ball's line of flight after racket contact.

Umpire: An individual responsible for officiating a tournament match.

Underspin: Same as *backspin.*

Unforced error: The loss of a point with no pressure having been exerted by the opponent.

United States Lawn Tennis Association (USLTA): The original governing body for tennis in the United States; known today as the United States Tennis Association.

United States Professional Tennis Association (USPTA): An organization of teaching professionals designed to promote ethical standards and sound educational methods for the sport.

United States Tennis Association (USTA): The governing body for tennis in the United States; formerly the United States Lawn Tennis Association (USLTA).

Van Alen Simplified Scoring System (VASSS): A scoring system whereby 21 or 31 points constitutes a set.

Volley: To hit a ball before it bounces; not applied to the serve.

Warm-up: The physical preparation immediately before a match, which generally consists of stretching exercises and stroke practice.

Western grip: The method of gripping a racket by forming a "V" with the thumb and index finger on the back plate. It is not a recommended grip due to the mechanical disadvantages it presents when hitting normal ground strokes.

Wide: Refers to balls landing out of bounds to the sides of the court.

Wightman Cup: Annual competition between female players of the United States and Great Britain; five singles and two doubles matches are played.

Wimbledon: A prestigious tournament held annually in England and considered to be one of the "Grand Slam" tournaments.

Women's Tennis Association (WTA): An organization of professional female tennis players.

Wood shot: Hitting a ball off the racket frame of a wooden racket.

World Championship Tennis (WCT): One of the early promoters of professional tennis throughout the world; currently sponsors a highly competitive circuit for men with extraordinary sums of prize money awarded.

World Tennis Association (WTA): An organization consisting of the world's best female professional players.

Comprehensive
Tennis Bibliography

Books

Addie, Pauline B. *Tennis for Teenagers.* Washington, D.C.: Pond, 1966.

Annarino, Anthony A. *Tennis.* Englewood Cliffs, New Jersey: Prentice-Hall, 1973.

Anthony, Julie. *A Winning Combination.* New York: Scribners, 1980.

Antonacci, Robert J. *Tennis For Young Champions.* New York: McGraw-Hill, 1982.

Arkinstall, Jack. *The Arkinstall Tennis Rhythm Method.* New York: Vantage Press, 1967.

Ashe, Arthur. *Arthur Ashe's Tennis Clinic.* New York: Simon and Simon, 1981.

Ashe, Arthur and Frank DeFord. *Arthur Ashe: Portrait in Motion.* Boston: Houghton Mifflin, 1975.

Barker, Sue. *Playing Tennis.* New York: Taplinger, 1979.

Barnaby, John M. *Advantage Tennis: Racket Work, Tactics, and Logic.* Boston: Allyn and Bacon, 1975.

_____. *Ground Strokes in Match Play: Techniques, Tempo, and Winning Tactics.* Garden City, New York: Doubleday, 1978.

Bartlett, Michael and Bob Gillen (Eds.). *The Tennis Book.* New York: Arbor House, 1981.

Bassett, Glenn. *Tennis: The Bassett System.* Chicago: Regnery, 1977.

Beasley, Mercer. *How to Improve Your Tennis.* New York: Home Institute, 1939.

Benjamin, David. *Competitive Tennis: A Guide for Parents and Young Players.* New York: J. B. Lippincott, 1979.

Book of Tennis: How to Play the Game. Edited by *World Tennis Magazine.* New York: Grosset and Dunlap, 1965.

Borg, Bjorn. *My Life and Game.* New York: Simon and Schuster, 1980.

Braden, Vic and Bill Bruns. *Teaching Children Tennis the Vic Braden Way.* Boston: Little, Brown, 1980.

_____. *Vic Braden's Tennis for the Future.* Boston: Little, Brown, 1977.

Bradlee, Dick. *Instant Tennis.* New York: Devin-Adair, 1962.

Brady, Maurice. *Lawn Tennis Encyclopedia.* South Brunswick, New Jersey: A. S. Barnes, 1969.

Brecheen, Joel. *Tennis Made Easy.* North Hollywood, California: Wilshire, 1974.

Brent, R. Spencer. *Pattern Play Tennis.* Garden City, New York: Doubleday, 1974.

Brown, Gene (Ed.). *Tennis.* New York: Arno Press, 1979.

Brown, Jim. *Tennis: Strokes, Strategy, and Programs.* Englewood Cliffs, New Jersey: Prentice-Hall, 1980.

_____. *Tennis: Teaching, Coaching, and Directing Programs.* Englewood Cliffs, New Jersey: Prentice-Hall, 1976.

_____. *Tennis Without Lessons.* Englewood Cliffs, New Jersey: Prentice-Hall, 1978.

Bruce, Ethel S., and Bert O. Bruce. *Tennis: Fundamentals and Timing.* New York: Prentice-Hall, 1938.

Budge, Donald J. *Budge on Tennis.* Englewood Cliffs, New Jersey: Prentice-Hall, 1939.

_____. *Tennis Made Easy.* New York: Ronald Press, 1945.

Buxton, Angela. *Tackle Lawn Tennis This Way.* New Rochelle, New Jersey: Sportshelf, 1958.

Campbell, Shep (Ed.). *Quick Tips from the CBS Tennis Spot.* New York: Simon and Schuster, 1981.

Casewit, Curtis W. *America's Tennis Book.* New York: Scribner, 1975.

Charles, Allegra. *How to Win at Ladies' Doubles.* New York: Arco, 1975.

Chase, Edward T. *Covering the Court.* Garden City, New York: Doubleday, 1976.

Collins, D. Ray and Patrick B. Hodges. *A Comprehensive Guide to Sports Skills Tests and Measurement.* Springfield, Illinois: Charles C Thomas, 1978.

Conroy, John J. *The Tennis Workbook: Unit II.* Englewood Cliffs, New Jersey: Scholastic Coach Book Services, 1969.

Court, Margaret S. *Court on Court: Life in Tennis.* New York: Dodd, Mead, 1975.

Cummings, Parke. *American Tennis.* Boston: Little, Brown, 1957.

Cutler, Merritt D. *The Tennis Book.* New York: McGraw-Hill, 1967.

_____. *Basic Tennis Illustrated.* New York: Dover, 1980.

Davies, Mike. *Lawn Tennis.* New York: Arc Books, 1962.

Davison-Lungley, Robin. *Let's Play Tennis*. London: Octopus Books, 1979.

Douglas, Paul. *The Handbook of Tennis*. New York: Knopf, 1982.

Driver, Helen I. *Tennis Self-Instructor*. Madison, Wisconsin: Monona-Driver, 1953.

_____. *Tennis for Teachers*. Philadelphia: W. B. Saunders, 1941.

_____. *Tennis for Teachers*. Madison, Wisconsin: Monona-Driver, 1964.

_____. *Tennis for Teachers* (2nd ed.). Madison, Wisconsin: Monona-Driver, 1970.

Duroska, Lud. *Tennis for Beginners*. New York: Grosset and Dunlap, 1975.

Durr, Francoise. *Doubles Strategy: A Creative and Psychological Approach to Tennis*. New York: David McKay, 1978.

Eldred, Vince. *Tennis Without Mistakes*. New York: Putnam, 1975.

Elliott, Bruce and Rob Kilderry. *The Art and Science of Tennis*. Philadelphia: Saunders College Publishing, 1983.

Etchebaster, Pierre. *Pierre's Book: The Game of Court Tennis*. Barre, Massachusetts: Barre Publishers, 1971.

Everett, Peter, and Virginia Skillman. *Beginning Tennis* (Rev. ed.). Belmont, California: Wadsworth, 1968.

Fannin, James. *Tennis and Kids: The Family Connection*. Garden City, New York: Doubleday, 1979.

Faulkner, Ed and F. Weymuller. *Tennis: How To Play It, How To Teach It*. New York: Dial Press, 1970.

Fiott, Steve. *Tennis Equipment*. Radnor, Pennsylvania: Chilton, 1978.

Fiske, Loring. *How to Beat Better Tennis Players*. Garden City, New York: Doubleday, 1970.

Fraley, Oscar. *How to Play Championship Tennis*. New York: A. A. Wyn, 1954.

Frasey, Neale. *Successful Tennis: From Beginner to Expert In Forty Lessons*. New York: Putnam, 1974.

Gallwey, W. Timothy. *The Inner Game of Tennis*. New York: Random House, 1974.

_____. *Inner Tennis*. New York: Random House, 1976.

Gensemer, Robert E. *Tennis*. Philadelphia: W. B. Saunders, 1969.

_____. *Tennis* (3rd ed.). Philadelphia: Saunders College Publishing, 1982.

Gillen, Bob (Ed.). *Winning Tennis: Strokes and Strategies of the World's Top Pros.* Radnor, Pennsylvania: Chilton, 1978.

Gimmy, Arthur E. *Tennis Clubs and Racquet Sports Projects.* Chicago: American Institute of Real Estate Appraisers of the National Association of Realtors, 1978.

Gonzales, Pancho. *Tennis.* New York: Avenel Books, 1962.

_____. *Tennis.* New York: Fleet, 1962.

_____. *Tennis Begins at Forty.* New York: Dial Press, 1976.

Gonzales, Pancho and Dick Hawk. *Tennis.* New York: Fleet, 1962.

Gonzales, Pancho and J. Hyams. *Winning Tactics for Weekend Singles.* New York: Bantam Books, 1974.

Gould, Dick. *Tennis Anyone?* (3rd ed.). Palo Alto, California: Mayfield, 1978.

Green, Robert E. *Tennis Drills.* New York: Hawthorn Books, 1976.

Grimsley, Will. *Tennis: Its History, People and Events.* Englewood Cliffs, New Jersey: Prentice-Hall, 1971.

Groppel, Jack L. *Optimal Tennis.* Chicago: Contemporary Books, 1983.

Gunter, Nancy R. et al. *Tennis for Women.* New York: Doubleday, 1973.

Harman, Bob and Keith Monroe. *Use Your Head in Tennis.* New York: Thomas Y. Crowell, 1975.

Hart, Doris. *Tennis With Hart.* Philadelphia: J. B. Lippincott, 1955.

Haynes, Connie. *Speed, Strength, and Stamina: Conditioning for Tennis.* Garden City, New York: Doubleday, 1975.

Heldman, Gladys and Cornel Lumiere. *The Book of Tennis.* New York: Grosset and Dunlap, 1965.

Herzog, Billy J. *Tennis Handbook.* Dubuque, Iowa: Kendall/Hunt, 1973.

_____. *Tennis Handbook* (2nd ed.). Dubuque, Iowa: Kendall/Hunt, 1975.

_____. *Tennis Handbook* (3rd ed.). Dubuque, Iowa: Kendall/Hunt, 1977.

Hillas, Marjorie. *Tennis.* Dubuque, Iowa: Wm. C. Brown, 1955.

Hopman, Harry. *Better Tennis for Boys and Girls.* New York: Dodd, Mead, 1972.

_____. *Lobbing Into the Sun.* Indianapolis: Bobbs Merrill, 1975.

Hovis, Ford (Ed.). *Tennis for Women.* Garden City, New York: Doubleday, 1980.

Huang, Bob. *Teaching Your Child Tennis.* Chicago: Contemporary Books, 1979.

Huss, Sally M. *How to Play Power Tennis With Ease.* New York: Harcourt, Brace, Jovanovich, 1979.

Jacobs, Helen H. *Tennis.* New York: A. S. Barnes, 1941.

Jaeger, Eloise M. *Teaching of Tennis for School and Recreational Programs.* Minneapolis: Burgess, 1963.

Johnson, Joan D. and Paul J. Xanthos. *Tennis.* Dubuque, Iowa: Wm. C. Brown, 1967.

_____. *Tennis* (2nd ed.). Dubuque, Iowa: Wm. C. Brown, 1972.

_____. *Tennis* (3rd ed.). Dubuque, Iowa: Wm. C. Brown, 1976.

_____. *Tennis* (4th ed.). Dubuque, Iowa: Wm. C. Brown, 1981.

Jones, Clarence M. *How to Play Tennis.* Secaucus, New Jersey: Chartwell Books, 1979.

_____. *Improving Your Tennis: Strokes and Techniques.* London: Faber and Faber, 1973.

_____. *Tennis: How to Become a Champion.* New York: Transatlantic Arts, 1968.

_____. *Tennis: How to Become a Champion.* London: Faber and Faber, 1970.

Keith, Harold. *Sports and Games.* New York: Thomas Y. Crowell, 1941.

Kenfield, John. *Teaching and Coaching Tennis.* Dubuque, Iowa: Wm. C. Brown, 1964.

King, Billie Jean. *Billie Jean King's Secrets of Winning Tennis.* New York: Holt, Rinehart and Winston, 1974.

_____. *How to Play Mixed Doubles.* New York: Simon and Schuster, 1980.

_____. *Tennis Love: A Parents Guide to the Sport.* New York: Macmillan, 1978.

King, Billie Jean and Kim Chapin. *Tennis to Win.* New York: Harper and Row, 1970.

Kraft, Steven (Ed.). *Tennis Drills for Self Improvement: Ten of the Nation's Top Young Tennis Coaches Offer Forty-Two Favorite Drills.* Garden City, New York: Doubleday, 1978.

Kraft, Virginia. *Tennis Instruction for Fun and Competition.* New York: Grosset and Dunlap, 1976.

Kramer, Jack. *How to Play Your Best Tennis All The Time.* New York: Atheneum, 1977.

LaMarche, Robert J. (Ed.). *Teach Yourself Tennis!* New York: Simon and Schuster, 1980.

Laney, Al. *Covering the Court: A 50-Year Love Affair With the Game of Tennis.* New York: Simon and Schuster, 1968.

Lardner, Rex. *The Complete Beginner's Guide to Tennis.* Garden City, New York: Doubleday, 1967.

_____. *Finding and Exploiting Your Opponent's Weaknesses.* Garden City, New York: Doubleday, 1978.

_____. *Tactics in Women's Singles, Doubles, and Mixed Doubles.* Garden City, New York: Doubleday, 1975.

Lardner, Rex. *The Underhanded Serve: Or How to Play Dirty Tennis.* New York: Hawthorn Books, 1968.

Laver, Rodney G. *How to Play Championship Tennis.* New York: Macmillan, 1965.

_____. *Rod Laver's Tennis Digest.* Northfield, Illinois: Digest Books, 1975.

_____. *Tennis for the Bloody Fun of It.* New York: Quadrangle/New York Times Book Company, 1976.

_____. *Tennis Guide.* Largo, Florida: Snibbe, 1970.

Laver, Rodney G. and Bud Collins (Eds.). *Rod Laver's Tennis Digest* (2nd ed.). Northfield, Illinois: Digest Books, 1978.

Leary, Don J. *The Teaching Tennis Pro.* Los Angeles: Pinnacle Books, 1979.

Leighton, Harry. *Junior Tennis.* New York: Sterling, 1974.

_____. *Tennis.* Chicago: Athletic Institute, 1953.

Leighton, Jim. *Inside Tennis: Techniques of Winning.* Englewood Cliffs, New Jersey: Prentice-Hall, 1977.

Litz, David. *A Photographic Guide to Tennis Fundamentals.* New York: Arco, 1978.

Lord, Sterling. *Returning the Serve Intelligently.* Garden City, New York: Doubleday, 1976.

Lott, George. *How to Play Winning Doubles.* New York: Simon and Schuster, 1979.

MacCurdy, Doug and Shawn Tully. *Sports Illustrated Tennis.* New York: J. B. Lippincott and Thomas Y Crowell, 1980.

Mace, Wynn. *Tennis Techniques Illustrated.* New York: Ronald Press, 1952.

Mason, Elaine R. *Tennis.* Boston: Allyn and Bacon, 1974.

McCormick, Bill. *Tennis.* New York: Watts, 1973.

McPhee, John A. *Wimbledon: A Celebration.* New York: Viking Press, 1972.

Mead, Shepherd. *How to Succeed in Tennis Without Really Trying.* New York: David McKay, 1977.

Metzler, Paul. *Advanced Tennis.* New York: Sterling, 1972.

_____. *Getting Started in Tennis.* New York: Sterling, 1972.

_____. *Tennis Doubles; Tactics and Formations.* New York: Sterling, 1975.

_____. *Tennis Styles and Stylists.* New York: Sterling, 1969.

_____. *Tennis Weaknesses and Remedies.* New York: Sterling, 1973.

Moore, Clancy and M. B. Chafin. *Tennis Everyone* (2nd ed.). Winston-Salem, North Carolina: Hunter, 1981.

Morton, Jason. *Winning Tennis After Forty.* Englewood Cliffs, New Jersey: Prentice-Hall, 1980.

Mottram, Anthony. *Improve Your Tennis.* Baltimore: Penguin Books, 1966.

_____. *Modern Lawn Tennis.* London: N. Kaye, 1957.

_____. *Play Better Tennis.* New York: Arco, 1971.

_____. *Skills and Tactics of Tennis.* New York: Arco, 1980.

Mulloy, Gardnar. *The Will to Win: An Inside View of the World of Tennis.* New York: A. S. Barnes, 1960.

Murphy, Chet. *Advanced Tennis.* Dubuque, Iowa: Wm. C. Brown, 1970.

_____. *Advanced Tennis* (2nd ed.). Dubuque, Iowa: Wm. C. Brown, 1976.

_____. *Advanced Tennis* (3rd ed.). Dubuque, Iowa: Wm. C. Brown, 1982.

Murphy, Chet and Bill Murphy. *Tennis for the Player, Teacher and Coach.* Philadelphia: W. B. Saunders, 1975.

Murphy, William E. *Complete Book of Championship Tennis Drills.* West Nyack, New York: Parker, 1975.

_____. *Lifetime Treasury of Tested Tennis Tips: Secrets of Winning Play.* West Nyack, New York: Parker, 1978.

Murphy, William E. and Chet Murphy. *Tennis for Beginners.* New York: Ronald Press, 1958.

_____. *Tennis Handbook.* New York: Ronald Press, 1962.

Navratilova, Martina. *Tennis My Way.* New York: Scribners, 1983.

Newcombe, John. *The Family Tennis Book.* New York: *Tennis Magazine* and *New York Times* Book Company, 1975.

Nickerson, Elinor. *Racquet Sports: An Illustrated Guide.* Jefferson, North Carolina: McFarland, 1982.

Official Encyclopedia of Tennis. United States Lawn Tennis Association. New York: Harper and Row, 1972.

Pasarell, Charlie. *Mastering Your Tennis Strokes.* New York: Atheneum, 1976.

Patterson, J. *How to Hit Two-Handed Backhands.* Tallahassee, Florida: A. B. Dick, 1976.

Pearce, Wayne. *Tennis.* Englewood Cliffs, New Jersey: Prentice-Hall, 1971.

Pelton, Barry C. *Tennis.* Pacific Palisades, California: Goodyear, 1969.

_____. *Tennis* (2nd ed.). Pacific Palisades, California: Goodyear, 1973.

Plagenhoef, Stanley C. *Fundamentals of Tennis.* Englewood Cliffs, New Jersey: Prentice-Hall, 1970.

Powell, Nick. *The Code.* Princeton, New Jersey: United States Lawn Tennis Association, 1974.

Ralston, Dennis. *Six Weeks to a Better Level of Tennis.* New York: Simon and Schuster, 1977.

Ramo, Simon. *Extraordinary Tennis for the Ordinary Player.* New York: Crown, 1977.

Richey, Nancy. *Tennis for Women.* Garden City, New York: Doubleday, 1980.

Riggs, Robert L. *Court Hustler.* Philadelphia: J. B. Lippincott, 1973.

Rosewall, Ken. *Ken Rosewall On Tennis.* New York: F. Fell, 1978.

Schultz, Nikki. *Tennis For Everyone.* New York: Grosset and Dunlap, 1974.

Schwed, Peter. *The Serve and the Overhead Smash.* Garden City, New York: Doubleday, 1976.

_____. *Sinister Tennis: How to Play Against and With Left-Handers.* Garden City, New York: Doubleday, 1975.

Scott, Eugene. *Tennis: Game of Motion.* New York: Crown, 1973.

Sebolt, Don R. *Tennis.* Dubuque, Iowa: Kendall/Hunt, 1970.

Sedgman, Frank. *Winning Tennis: The Australian Way to a Better Game.* New York: Prentice-Hall, 1954.

Segura, Pancho. *Pancho Segura's Championship Strategy: How to Play Winning Tennis.* New York: McGraw-Hill, 1976.

Seixas, Vic. *Prime Time Tennis.* New York: Scribner, 1983.

Shannon, Bill (Ed.). *United States Tennis Association Official Encyclopedia of Tennis.* New York: Harper and Row, 1981.

Sheehan, Larry (Ed.). *Mastering Your Tennis Strokes.* New York: Atheneum, 1976.

Singleton, John D. *How to Increase Your Net Value: A Simplified Guide to Better Tennis.* New York: Winchester Press, 1975.

Smith, Stanely R. *Inside Tennis.* Chicago: Regnery, 1974.

_____. *Stan Smith's Guide to Better Tennis.* New York: Grosset and Dunlap, 1975.

Snyder, Dave. *Tennis.* Chicago: Athletic Institute, 1971.

Soules, George. *The Playboy Book of Tennis: How to Play Winning Tennis and Everything Else You Forgot to Ask Your Pro.* New York: Playboy Press, 1982.

Talbert, William F. *Bill Talbert's Weekend Tennis: How to Have Fun and Win at the Same Time.* Garden City, New York: Doubleday, 1970.

_____. *Sports Illustrated Book of Tennis* (Rev. ed.). Philadelphia: J. B. Lippincott, 1972.

_____. *Tennis Tactics: Singles and Doubles.* New York: Harper and Row, 1983.

Talbert, William F. and Bruce S. Old. *The Game of Doubles in Tennis* (3rd ed.). Philadelphia: J. B. Lippincott, 1968.

_____. *The Game of Singles in Tennis.* Philadelphia: J. B. Lippincott, 1977.

_____. *Stroke Production in the Game of Tennis.* Philadelphia: J. B. Lippincott, 1971.

Tennis: How to Play How to Win. Editors of *Tennis Magazine.* New York: Simon and Schuster, 1978.

Tennis Group Instruction. USLTA-AAHPER Joint Committee. Washington, D.C.: American Association for Health, Physical Education and Recreation, 1963.

The Tennis Player's Handbook: A Buyer's Guide and Service Directory. Editors of *Tennis Magazine.* New York: Simon and Schuster, 1980.

Tennis Strokes and Strategies. Editors of *Tennis Magazine.* New York: Simon and Schuster, 1975.

Tilden, William T. *Singles and Doubles.* New York: George H. Doran, 1923.

Tilmanis, Gundars A. *Advanced Tennis for Coaches, Teachers and Players.* Philadelphia: Lea and Febiger, 1975.

Tingay, Lance. *The Guinness Book of Tennis Facts and Feats.* New York: Sterling, 1983.

_____. *Tennis: A Pictorial History.* New York: G. P. Putnam's Sons, 1973.

Trengove, Alan (Ed.). *How to Play Tennis the Professional Way.* New York: Simon and Schuster, 1964.

Tuckey, Charles. *Lawn Tennis for Men.* New York: M. S. Mill, 1937.

Van der Meer, Dennis. *Dennis Van der Meer's Complete Book of Tennis.* New York: Hawthorn Books, 1982.

Van der Meer, Dennis and Murray Olderman. *Tennis Clinic.* New York: Hawthorn Books, 1974.

Varn, Ben and Hank Jungle. *Stairsteps to Successful Tennis.* Travelers Rest, South Carolina: Tennis Services, 1974.

Vines, Ellsworth. *Tennis: Myth and Method.* New York: Viking Press, 1978.

Whitington, Richard S. *An Illustrated History of Australian Tennis.* New York: St. Martin's Press, 1976.

Wilson, Craig R. *Tennis: Beyond the Inner Game.* New York: Drake, 1976.

Winnett, Tom. *Tennis is an Unnatural Act.* Berkeley, California: Wilderness Press, 1977.

Yale, Virginia. *Solo Tennis.* New York: Drake, 1976.

Periodicals

Black Tennis Magazine. Published quarterly by the Tennis Foundation of North America, 475 Riverside Drive, Suite 439, New York, New York 10015.

International Tennis Weekly. Published weekly by the Association of Tennis Professionals, P.O. Box 58085, World Trade Center, Dallas, Texas 75228.

Tennis Illustrated. Published monthly by the Devonshire Publications Company, 630 Shatto Place, Los Angeles, California 90005.

Tennis Industry. Published monthly by Industry Publishers, Incorporated, 1545 N.E. 123rd Street, North Miami, Florida 33161.

Tennis: Magazine of the Racquet Sports. Published monthly by Tennis Features, Incorporated, 495 Westport Avenue, Norwalk, Connecticut 06856 (Official publication of USPTA).

Tennis USA. Published monthly by Chilton Company, Chilton Way, Radnor, Pennsylvania 19089 (Official publication of USTA).

USTA Yearbook. Published annually by H. O. Zimman, Incorporated, 156 Broad Street, Lynn, Massachusetts 01901 (Official publication of USTA).

World Tennis. Published monthly by CBS Publications, the Consumer Publishing Division of CBS Incorporated, 1515 Broadway, New York, New York 10036 (Magazine for membership of USTA).

Appendix

TENNIS ORGANIZATIONS

UNITED STATES TENNIS ASSOCIATION (USTA)
51 East 42nd Street
New York, New York 10036

The USTA is the national governing body for tennis in the United States and is a member of the International Tennis Federation, with the expressed purpose of:

1. promoting the development of tennis as a means of healthful recreation and physical fitness;
2. establishing and maintaining rules of play and high standards of amateurism and good sportsmanship;
3. fostering national and international amateur tennis tournaments;
4. encouraging, sanctioning and conducting tennis tournaments and competititions;
5. assisting with the development of health, character and responsible citizenship.

Formerly known as the United States Lawn Tennis Association, the organization removed the word "lawn" from its title in 1975. The USTA encompasses all fifty states and is divided into four geographical regions comprised of seventeen sections. Your local and state tennis tournaments are affiliated with one of these sections.

USTA Sectional Names and Addresses

Eastern Tennis Association
180 East Post Road, Room 207
White Plains, New York 10601

Florida Tennis Association
520 N.E. 118th Street
Biscayne Park, Florida 33161

Hawaii Tennis Association
Box 411
Honolulu, Hawaii 96809

Intermountain Tennis Association
Box 6740
Denver, Colorado 80206

Middle Atlantic Tennis Association
5656 Ravenel Lane
Springfield, Virginia 22151

Middle State Tennis Association
Love Road R.D. 1
Box 146
Reading, Pennsylvania 19607

Missouri Valley Tennis Association
5727 Manchester
St. Louis, Missouri 63110

New England Tennis Association
Box 223
Needham, Massachusetts 02192

Northern California Tennis Association
Box 337
Morada, California 94556

Northwestern Tennis Association
3769 Towndale Drive
Bloomington, Minnesota 55431

Pacific Northwest Tennis Association
Box 02322
Portland, Oregon 97202

Puerto Rico Tennis Association
Box 40456
Minillas Station
Santurce, Puerto Rico 00940

Southern California Tennis Association
609 North Cahuenga Boulevard
Los Angeles, California 90004

Southern Tennis Association
3121 Maple Drive N.E.
Room 21B
Atlanta, Georgia 30305

Southwestern Tennis Association
1735 Rita N.E.
Albuquerque, New Mexico 87106

Texas Tennis Association
Box 192
Austin, Texas 78767

Western Tennis Association
1024 Torrence Drive
Springfield, Ohio 45503

USTA EDUCATION AND RESEARCH CENTER
729 Alexander Road
Princeton, New Jersey 08540
   A centralized facility of the USTA for providing assistance and materials related to membership, publications, films, video tapes, workshops, clinicians' service, speakers' bureau, facilities, plus other special areas related to tennis.

AMERICAN TENNIS ASSOCIATION (ATA)
   An active tennis organization for amateur black tennis players, started in 1916.

ASSOCIATION OF TENNIS PROFESSIONALS (ATP)
   A tennis association comprised of male playing professionals.

INTERNATIONAL RACQUET SPORTS ASSOCIATION (IRSA)

INTERNATIONAL TENNIS FEDERATION (ITF)
   An expansive tennis organization that represents the governing body of international tennis, including the USTA.

NATIONAL PUBLIC PARKS TENNIS ASSOCIATION (NPPTA)
   A nationwide tennis organization that is administered by municipal and county recreation departments.

NATIONAL TENNIS ASSOCIATION (NTA)

SENIOR WOMEN'S TENNIS ASSOCIATION (SWTA)
   An organization for the promotion of female senior tennis players.

SUPER SENIOR TENNIS (SST)
   An organization for the promotion of male senior tennis players over the age of 55.

UNITED STATES PROFESSIONAL TENNIS ASSOCIATION (USPTA)
   An organization for the promotion of teaching professionals that is designed to establish sound educational methods of instruction.

WOMEN'S TENNIS ASSOCIATION (WTA)
   A tennis association comprised of female playing professionals (counterpart of ATP).

WORLD CHAMPIONSHIP TENNIS (WCT)
   An organization that arranges tournaments throughout the world for professionals as a profit-making venture.

MAJOR COMPETITION

   Historically, all major tournaments or types of team competition were initially designed for amateur players. Over the years, as the professional players established their associations and playing circuits, it became increasingly difficult to attract top amateurs. The result has been that all major tournaments (team and individual) are now open to both amateurs and professionals.

Team Competition

Davis Cup. Competition for male players that was started in 1900 as a series between the United States and England. It now involves between 25 and 30 countries competing annually for the large silver trophy initially donated by Dwight Davis. Dual matches consisting of four singles and one doubles event are held against countries in the same zone, with the zone winners having a playoff. Each match is the best of five sets, with the victorious nation winning the best of five matches.

Federation Cup. Competition initiated by the International Tennis Federation in 1963 as international team play for females. A team match consists of two singles and one doubles event, with the winning nation taking the best of the three and advancing to the next round.

Wightman Cup. Competition for female players that was initiated in 1923 as a parallel to the Davis Cup format. The series is between the United States and England with the winner receiving a trophy donated by Hazel Wightman. This annual competition is held at alternating sites and consists of five singles and two doubles matches. At least four players are required to compete, and the nation taking the best of seven matches is the winner.

World Cup. Competition started in 1969 and designed to pit top players from the United States against those from other countries. The dual match consists of five singles and two doubles matches (best of seven), and competition thus far has been between the United States and Australia.

Individual Competition

The "Grand Slam" in tennis involves winning all four of the major international single elimination tournaments held annually. All four are "open" events for both male and female players. They include the All-England Championships (Wimbledon), the United States Open Championships, the French Championships and the Australian Championships.

In addition to the Grand Slam tournaments, individual players may choose to compete on one of the following circuits.

Grand Prix. An elaborate and complex year-round circuit of both male and female players that began in 1970 and includes both the Grand Slam and the World Championship tennis circuit competition. The Men's International Professional Tennis Council administers the tournaments, and they are also in charge of cumulative point totals and related prize money.

Virginia Slims. A circuit of professional female players that was established in 1970.

World Championship Tennis. A circuit of professional male players that was established in 1971.

RATING SCALE*

Through the years, commonly asked questions about tennis include, "What is my skill level?" "Should I consider myself to be a novice, beginner, intermediate or advanced player, or an A, B or C level player?" Fortunately, the International Racquet Sports Association has worked in close collaboration with the United States Professional Tennis Association and the United States Tennis Association to make available to the tennis-playing public a simplified self-rating program, known as the National Tennis Rating Program. The primary goal of the program is to help all tennis players enjoy the game by providing a method of classifying skill levels for more compatible matches, group lessons, league play, tournaments and other programs. The National Tennis Rating Program is based on the premise that any placement program must be easy to administer and be free, noncommercial and nonexclusive in order to be universally accepted and effective.

This program provides a simple, initial self-placement method of grouping individuals of similar ability levels for league play, tournaments, group lessons, social competition and club or community programs. The rating categories are generalizations about skill levels. You may find that you actually play above or below the category that best describes your skill level, depending on your competitive ability. The category you choose is not meant to be permanent but may be adjusted as your skills change or as your match play demonstrates the need for reclassification. Ultimately, your rating is based upon your results in match play.

To place yourself:

1. Begin with 1.0 (see the following rating categories). Read all categories carefully and then decide which one best describes your present ability level.

2. Be certain that you qualify on all points of all preceding categories as well as those in the classification you choose.

3. When rating yourself, assume you are playing against a player of the same sex and the same ability.

4. Your self-rating may be verified by a teaching professional, coach, league coordinator or other qualified expert.

5. The person in charge of your tennis program has the right to reclassify you if your self-placement is thought to be inappropriate based upon match results.

NTRP Rating Categories

1.0 This player is just starting to play tennis.

1.5 This player has limited playing experience and is still working primarily on getting the ball over the net; has some knowledge of scoring but is not familiar with basic positions and procedures for singles and doubles play.

2.0   This player may have had some lessons but needs on-court experience; has obvious stroke weaknesses but is beginning to feel comfortable with singles and doubles play.

2.5   This player has more dependable strokes and is learning to judge where the ball is going; has weak court coverage or is often caught out of position, but is starting to keep the ball in play with other players of the same ability.

3.0   This player can place shots with moderate success; can sustain a rally of slow pace but is not comfortable with all strokes; lacks control when trying for power.

3.5   This player has achieved stroke dependability and direction on shots within reach, including forehand and backhand volleys, but still lacks depth and variety; seldom double faults and occasionally forces errors on the serve.

4.0   This player has dependable strokes on both forehand and backhand sides; has the ability to use a variety of shots, including lobs, overheads, approach shots and volleys; can place the first serve and force some errors; is seldom out of position in a doubles game.

4.5   This player has begun to master the use of power and spins; has sound footwork; can control depth of shots and is able to move opponent up and back; can hit first serves with power and accuracy and place the second serve; is able to rush net with some success on serve in singles as well as doubles.

5.0   This player has good shot anticipation; frequently has an outstanding shot or exceptional consistency around which a game may be structured; can regularly hit winners or force errors off of shot balls; can successfully execute lobs, drop shots, half volleys and smashes; has good depth and spin on most second serves.

5.5   This player can execute all strokes offensively and defensively; can hit dependable shots under pressure; is able to analyze opponent's styles and can employ patterns of play to assure the greatest possibility of winning points; can hit winners or force errors with both first and second serves. Return of serve can be an offensive weapon.

6.0   This player has mastered all of the above skills; has developed power and/or consistency as a major weapon; can vary strategies and styles of play in a competitive situation. This player typically has had intensive training for national competition at junior or collegiate levels.

6.5   This player has mastered all of the above skills and is an experienced tournament competitor who regularly travels for competition and whose income may be partially derived from prize winnings.

7.0   This is a world class player. Variations are measured by computerized rankings.

Based on the National Tennis Rating Program, the following classification system is suggested for rating tennis activity class participants and varsity performers in high school and college.

Beginner: 1.0–2.0
Intermediate: 2.5–3.0
Advanced: 3.5–4.0
Interscholastic: 4.5–?
Intercollegiate: 4.5–?

*USTA, IRSA, USPTA, 1979 (revised 1981, 1983)
Reprinted by permission of the USTA.

RULES OF TENNIS AND
CASES AND DECISIONS — 1984*

The following Rules and Cases and Decisions are the official Code of the International Tennis Federation, of which the United States Tennis Association is a member. USTA Comments and USTA Cases and Decisions have the same weight and force in USTA tournaments as do ITF Cases and Decisions.

When a match is played without officials the principles and guidelines set forth in the USTA Publication, The Code, shall apply in any situation not covered by the rules.

Except where otherwise stated, every reference in these Rules to the masculine includes the feminine gender.

A vertical line in the margin indicates a change or amendment made by the ITF at their Annual General Meeting in June 1983, and which took effect January 1, 1984.

The Singles Game
RULE 1

The Court

The court shall be a rectangle 78 feet (23.77m.) long and 27 feet (8.23m.) wide. **USTA Comment:** See Rule 34 for a doubles court.

It shall be divided across the middle by a net suspended from a cord or metal cable of a maximum diameter of one-third of an inch (0.8cm.), the ends of which shall be attached to, or pass over, the tops of two posts, which shall be not more than 6 inches (15cm.) square or 6 inches (15cm.) in diameter. The centres of the posts shall be 3 feet (0.914m.) outside the court on each side and the height of the posts shall be such that the top of the cord or metal cable shall be 3 feet 6 inches (1.07m.) above the ground.

When a combined doubles (see Rule 34) and singles court with a doubles net is used for singles, the net must be supported to a height of 3 feet 6 inches (1.07m.) by means of two posts, called "singles sticks", which shall be not more than 3 inches (7.5cm.) square or 3 inches (7.5cm.) in diameter. The centres of the singles sticks shall be 3 feet (0.914m.) outside the singles court on each side.

The net shall be extended fully so that it fills completely the space between the two posts and shall be of sufficiently small mesh to prevent the ball passing through. The height of the net shall be 3 feet (0.914m) at the centre, where it shall be held down taut by a strap not more than 2 inches (5cm.) wide and completely white in colour. There shall be a band covering the cord or metal cable and the top of the net of not less than 2 inches (5cm.) nor more than two and a half inches (6.3cm.) in depth on each side and completely white in colour.

There shall be no advertisement on the net, strap, band or singles sticks.

The lines bounding the ends and sides of the Court shall respectively be called the base-lines and the side-lines. On each side of the net, at a distance of 21 feet (6.40m.) from it and parallel with it, shall be drawn the service-lines. The space on each side of the net between the service-line and the side-lines shall be divided into two equal parts called the service-courts by the centre service-line, which must be 2 inches (5cm.) in width, drawn half-way between, and parallel with, the side-lines. Each base-line shall be bisected by an imaginary continuation of the centre service-line to a line 4 inches (10cm.) in length and 2 inches (5cm.) in width called the centre mark drawn inside the Court, at right angles to and in contact with such base-lines. All other lines shall be not less than 1 inch (2.5cm.) nor more than 2 inches (5cm.) in width, except the base-line, which may be 4 inches (10cm.) in width, and all measurements shall be made to the outside of the lines. All lines shall be of uniform colour.

If advertising or any other material is placed at the back of the court, it may not contain white or yellow, or any other light colour.

If advertisements are placed on the chairs of the Linesmen sitting at the back of the court, they may not contain white or yellow.

Note: In the case of the International Tennis Championship (Davis Cup) or other Official Championships of the International Tennis Federation, there shall be a space behind each baseline of not less than 21 feet (6.4m.), and at the sides of not less than 12 feet (3.66m.).

USTA Comment: *It is important to have a stick 3 feet, 6 inches long, with a notch cut in at the 3-foot mark for the purpose of measuring the height of the net at the posts and in the center. These measurements always should be made before starting to play a match.*

RULE 2
Permanent Fixtures

The permanent fixtures of the Court shall include not only the net, posts, singles sticks, cord or metal cable, strap and band, but also, where there are any such, the back and side stops, the stands, fixed or movable seats and chairs round the Court, and their occupants, all other fixtures around and above the Court, and the Umpire, Net-cord Judge, Foot-fault Judge, Linesmen and Ball Boys when in their respective places.

Note: For the purpose of this Rule, the word "Umpire" comprehends the Umpire, the persons entitled to a seat on the Court, and all those persons designated to assist the Umpire in the conduct of a match.

RULE 3
The Ball

The ball shall have a uniform outer surface and shall be white or yellow in colour. If there are any seams, they shall be stitchless.

The ball shall be more than two and a half inches (6.35cm.) and less than two and five-eighths inches (6.67cm.) in diameter, and more than two ounces (56.7 grams) and less than two and one-sixteenth ounces (58.5 grams) in weight.

The ball shall have a bound of more than 53 inches (135cm.) and less than 58 inches (147cm.) when dropped 100 inches (254cm.) upon a concrete base.

The ball shall have a forward deformation of more than .220 of an inch (.56cm.) and less than .290 of an inch (.74cm.) and a return deformation of more than .350 of an inch (.89cm.) and less than .425 of an inch (1.08cm.) at 18 lb. (8.165kg.) load. The two deformation figures shall be the averages of three individual readings along three axes of the ball and no two individual readings shall differ by more than .030 of an inch (.08cm.) in each case.

All tests for bound, size and deformation shall be made in accordance with the Regulations in the Appendix hereto.

RULE 4
The Racket
Rackets failing to comply with the following specifications are not approved for play under the Rules of Tennis:

(a) The hitting surface of the racket shall be flat and consist of a pattern of crossed strings connected to a frame and alternately interlaced or bonded where they cross; and the stringing pattern shall be generally uniform, and in particular not less dense in the centre than in any other area.

(b) The frame of the racket shall not exceed 32 inches (81.28cm.) in overall length, including the handle and 12½ inches (31.75cm.) in overall width. The strung surface shall not exceed 15½ inches (39.37cm.) in overall length, and 11½ inches (29.21cm.) in overall width.

(c) The frame, including the handle, and the strings:

(i) shall be free of attached objects and protrusions, other than those utilised solely and specifically to limit or prevent wear and tear or vibration, or to distribute weight, and which are reasonable in size and placement for such purposes; and

(ii) shall be free of any device which makes it possible for a player to change materially the shape of the racket.

The International Tennis Federation shall rule on the question of whether any racket or prototype complies with the above specifications or is otherwise approved, or not approved, for play. Such ruling may be undertaken on its own initiative, or upon application by any party with a bona fide interest therein, including any player, equipment manufacturer or National Association or members thereof. Such rulings and applications shall be made in accordance with the applicable Review and Hearing Procedures of the International Tennis Federation, copies of which may be obtained from the office of the Secretary.

RULE 5
Server and Receiver
The players shall stand on opposite sides of the net; the player who

first delivers the ball shall be called the Server, and the other the Receiver.

Case 1. Does a player, attempting a stroke, lose the point if he crosses an imaginary line in the extension of the net,

    (a) before striking the ball,

    (b) after striking the ball?

Decision. He does not lose the point in either case by crossing the imaginary line and provided he does not enter the lines bounding his opponent's Court (Rule 20 (e)). In regard to hindrance, his opponent may ask for the decision of the Umpire under Rules 21 and 25.

Case 2. The Server claims that the Receiver must stand within the lines bounding his Court. Is this necessary?

Decision. No. The Receiver may stand wherever he pleases on his own side of the net.

RULE 6

Choice of Ends and Service

The choice of ends and the right to be Server or Receiver in the first game shall be decided by toss. The player winning the toss may choose or require his opponent to choose:

(a) The right to be Server or Receiver, in which case the other player shall choose the end; or

(b) The end, in which case the other player shall choose the right to be Server or Receiver.

USTA Comment: *These choices should be made promptly and are irrevocable.*

RULE 7

The Service

The service shall be delivered in the following manner. Immediately before commencing to serve, the Server shall stand with both feet at rest behind (i.e. further from the net than) the base-line, and within the imaginary continuations of the centre-mark and side-line. The Server shall then project the ball by hand into the air in any direction and before it hits the ground strike it with his racket, and the delivery shall be deemed to have been completed at the moment of the impact of the racket and the ball. A player with the use of only one arm may utilize his racket for the projection.

USTA Comment: *The service begins when the Server takes a ready position and ends when his racket makes contact with the ball, or when he misses the ball in attempting to serve it.*

Case 1. May the Server in a singles game take his stand behind the portion of the base-line between the side-lines of the Singles Court and the Doubles Court?

Decision. No.

Case 2. If a player, when serving, throws up two or more balls instead of one, does he lose that service?

Decision. No. A let should be called, but if the Umpire regards the action as deliberate he may take action under Rule 21.

USTA Case 3. May a player serve underhand?

Decision. Yes. There is no restriction regarding the kind of service which may be used; that is, the player may use an underhand or overhand service at his discretion.

RULE 8

Foot Fault

The Server shall throughout the delivery of the service:

(a) Not change his position by walking or running.

(b) Not touch, with either foot, any area other than that behind the base-line within the imaginary extensions of the centre mark and side-lines.

Note: The following interpretation of Rule 8 was approved by the International Tennis Federation on 9th July, 1958:

(a) The Server shall not, by slight movements of the feet which do not materially affect the location originally taken up by him, be deemed "to change his position by walking or running".

(b) The word "foot" means the extremity of the leg below the ankle.

USTA Comment: *This rule covers the most decisive stroke in the game, and there is no justification for its not being obeyed by players and enforced by officials. No official has the right to instruct any umpire to disregard violations of it. In a non-officiated match, it is the prerogative of the Receiver, or his partner, to call foot faults, but only after all efforts (appeal to the server, requests for an umpire, etc.) have failed, and the foot faulting is so flagrant as to be clearly perceptible from the Receiver's side.*

RULE 9
Delivery of Service

(a) In delivering the service, the Server shall stand alternately behind the right and left Courts beginning from the right in every game. If service from a wrong half of the Court occurs and is undetected, all play resulting from such wrong service or services shall stand, but the inaccuracy of station shall be corrected immediately it is discovered.

(b) The ball served shall pass over the net and hit the ground within the Service Court which is diagonally opposite, or upon any line bounding such Court, before the Receiver returns it.

RULE 10
Service Fault

The Service is a fault:

(a) If the Server commits any breach of Rules 7, 8 or 9;

(b) If he misses the ball in attempting to strike it;

(c) If the ball served touches a permanent fixture (other than the net, strap or band) before it hits the ground.

Case 1. After throwing a ball up preparatory to serving, the Server decides not to strike at it and catches it instead. Is it a fault?

Decision. No. **USTA Comment:** As long as the Server makes no attempt to strike the ball, it is immaterial whether he catches it in his hand or racket or lets it drop to the ground.

Case 2. In serving in a singles game played on a Doubles Court with doubles posts and singles sticks, the ball hits a singles stick and then hits the ground within the lines of the correct Service Court. Is this a fault or a let?

Decision. In serving it is a fault, because the singles stick, the doubles post, and that portion of the net, or band between them are permanent fixtures. (Rules 2 and 10, and note to Rule 24.).

USTA Comment: *The significant point governing Case 2 is that the part of the net and band "outside" the singles sticks is not part of the net over which this singles match is being played. Thus such a serve is a fault under the provisions of Article (c) above... By the same token, this would be a fault also if it were a singles game played with permanent posts in the singles position. (See Case 1 under Rule 24 for difference between "service" and "good return" with respect to a ball's hitting a net post.)*

USTA Comment: *In matches played without umpires each player makes calls för all balls hit to his side of the net. In doubles, normally the Receiver's partner makes the calls with respect to the service line, with the Receiver calling the side and center lines, but either partner may make the call on any ball he clearly sees out.*

RULE 11

Second Service

After a fault (if it is the first fault) the Server shall serve again from behind the same half of the Court from which he served that fault, unless the service was from the wrong half, when, in accordance with Rule 9, the Server shall be entitled to one service only from behind the other half.

Case 1. A player serves from a wrong Court. He loses the point and then claims it was a fault because of his wrong station.

Decision. The point stands as played and the next service should be from the correct station according to the score.

Case 2. The point score being 15 all, the Server, by mistake, serves from the left-hand Court. He wins the point. He then serves again from the right-hand Court, delivering a fault. This mistake in station is then discovered. Is he entitled to the previous point? From which Court should he next serve?

Decision. The previous point stands. The next service should be from the left-hand Court, the score being 30/15, and the Server has served one fault.

RULE 12

When To Serve

The Server shall not serve until the Receiver is ready. If the latter attempts to return the service, he shall be deemed ready. If, however, the Receiver signifies that he is not ready, he may not claim a fault because the ball does not hit the ground within the limits fixed for the service.

USTA Comment: *The Server must wait until the Receiver is ready for the second service as well as the first, and if the Receiver claims to be not ready and does not make any effort to return a service, the Server may not claim the point, even though the service was good.*

RULE 13

The Let

In all cases where a let has to be called under the rules, or to provide for an interruption to play, it shall have the following interpretations:

(a) When called solely in respect of a service that one service only shall be replayed.

(b) When called under any other circumstance, the point shall be replayed.

USTA Comment: *A service that touches the net in passing yet falls into the proper court (or touches the receiver) is a let. This word is used also when, because of an interruption while the ball is in play, or for any other reason, a point is to be replayed. A spectator's outcry (of "out", "fault" or other) is not a valid basis for replay of a point, but action should be taken to prevent a recurrence.*

`Case 1.* A service is interrupted by some cause outside those defined in Rule 14. Should the service only be replayed?
Decision. No, the whole point must be replayed.

USTA Comment: *The phrase "in respect of a service" in (a) means a let because a served ball has touched the net before landing in the proper court, OR because the Receiver was not ready... Case 1 refers to a second serve, and the decision means that if the interruption occurs during delivery of the second service, the Server gets two serves. Example: On a second service a linesman calls "fault" and immediately corrects it (the Receiver meanwhile having let the ball go by). The Server is entitled to two serves, on this ground: The corrected call means that the Server has put the ball into play with a good service, and once the ball is in play and a let is called, the point must be replayed... Note, however, that if the serve is an unmistakable ace — that is, the Umpire is sure the erroneous call had no part in the Receiver's inability to play the ball — the point should be declared for the Server.*

Case 2. If a ball in play becomes broken, should a let be called?
Decision. Yes.

USTA Comment: *A ball shall be regarded as having become "broken" if, in the opinion of the Chair Umpire, it is found to have lost compression to the point of being unfit for further play, or unfit for any reason, and it is clear the defective ball was the one in play.*

RULE 14

The "Let" in Service

The service is a let:

(a) If the ball served touches the net, strap or band, and is otherwise good, or, after touching the net, strap or band, touches the Receiver or anything which he wears or carries before hitting the ground.

(b) If a service or a fault is delivered when the Receiver is not ready (see Rule 12).

In case of a let, that particular service shall not count, and the Server shall serve again, but a service let does not annul a previous fault.

RULE 15

Order of Service

At the end of the first game the Receiver shall become Server, and the Server Receiver; and so on alternately in all the subsequent games of a match. If a player serves out of turn, the player who ought to have served shall serve as soon as the mistake is discovered, but all points scored before such discovery shall be reckoned. If a game shall have been completed before such discovery, the order of service remains as altered. A fault served before such discovery shall not be reckoned.

RULE 16

When Players Change Ends

The players shall change ends at the end of the first, third and every subsequent alternate game of each set, and at the end of each set unless the total number of games in such set is even, in which case the change is not made until the end of the first game of the next set.

If a mistake is made and the correct sequence is not followed the players must take up their correct station as soon as the discovery is made and follow their original sequence.

RULE 17

The Ball In Play

A ball is in play from the moment at which it is delivered in service. Unless a fault or a let is called it remains in play until the point is decided.

USTA Comment: *A point is not "decided" simply when, or because, a good shot has clearly passed a player, or when an apparently bad shot passes over a baseline or sideline. An outgoing ball is still definitely "in play" until it actually strikes the ground, backstop or a permanent fixture, or a player. The same applies to a good ball, bounding after it has landed in the proper court. A ball that becomes imbedded in the net is out of play.*

Case 1. A player fails to make a good return. No call is made and the ball remains in play. May his opponent later claim the point after the rally has ended?

Decision. No. The point may not be claimed if the players continue to play after the error has been made, provided the opponent was not hindered.

USTA Comment: *To be valid, an out call on A's shot to B's court, that B plays, must be made before B's return has either gone out of play or has been hit by A. See Case 3 under Rule 29.*

USTA Case 2. A ball is played into the net; the player on the other side, thinking that the ball is coming over, strikes at it and hits the net. Who loses the point?

Decision. If the player touched the net while the ball was still in play, he loses the point.

RULE 18

Server Wins Point

The Server wins the point:

(a) If the ball served, not being a let under Rule 14, touches the Receiver or anything which he wears or carries, before it hits the ground;

(b) If the Receiver otherwise loses the point as provided by Rule 20.

RULE 19

Receiver Wins Point

The Receiver wins the point:

(a) If the Server serves two consecutive faults;

(b) If the Server otherwise loses the point as provided by Rule 20.

RULE 20

Player Loses Point

A player loses the point if:

(a) He fails, before the ball in play has hit the ground twice consecutively, to return it directly over the net (except as provided in Rule 24(a) or (c)); or

(b) He returns the ball in play so that it hits the ground, a permanent fixture, or other object, outside any of the lines which bound his opponent's Court (except as provided in Rule 24(a) or (c)); or

USTA Comment: *A ball hitting a scoring device or other object attached to a net post results in loss of point to the striker.*

(c) He volleys the ball and fails to make a good return even when standing outside the Court; or

(d) In playing the ball he deliberately carries or catches it on his racket or deliberately touches it with his racket more than once; or

USTA Comment: *Only when there is a definite "second push" by the player does his shot become illegal, with consequent loss of point. It should be noted that the word "deliberately" is the key word in this Rule and that two hits occurring in the course of a single continuous stroke would not be deemed a double hit.*

(e) He or his racket (in his hand or otherwise) or anything which he wears or carries touches the net, posts, singles sticks, cord or metal cable, strap or band, or the ground within his opponent's Court at any time while the ball is in play; or

USTA Comment: *Touching a pipe support that runs across the court at the bottom of the net is interpreted as touching the net; See USTA Comment under Rule 23.*

(f) He volleys the ball before it has passed the net; or

(g) The ball in play touches him or anything that he wears or carries, except his racket in his hand or hands; or

USTA Comment: *This loss of point occurs regardless of whether the player is inside or outside the bounds of his court when the ball touches him. Except for a ball used in a first service fault, a player is considered to be "wearing or carrying" anything that he was wearing*

or carrying at the beginning of the point during which the touch occurred. Exception: If an object worn or carried by a player falls to the ground and a ball hit by his opponent hits that object, then (1) if the ball falls outside the court, the opponent loses the point; (2) if the ball falls inside the court, a let is to be called.

(h) He throws his racket at and hits the ball; or

(i) He deliberately and materially changes the shape of his racket during the playing of the point.

Case 1. In delivering a first service which falls outside the proper Court, the Server's racket slips out of his hand and flies into the net. Does he lose the point?

Decision. If his racket touches the net whilst the ball is in play, the Server loses the point (Rule 20 *(e)*).

Case 2. In serving, the racket flies from the Server's hand and touches the net before the ball has touched the ground. Is this a fault, or does the player lose the point?

Decision. The Server loses the point because his racket touches the net whilst the ball is in play (Rule 20 *(e)*).

Case 3. A and B are playing against C and D, A is serving to D, C touches the net before the ball touches the ground. A fault is then called because the service falls outside the Service Court. Do C and D lose the point?

Decision. The call "fault" is an erroneous one. C and D had already lost the point before "fault" could be called, because C touched the net whilst the ball was in play (Rule 20 *(e)*).

Case 4. May a player jump over the net into his opponent's Court while the ball is in play and not suffer penalty?

Decision. No. He loses the point (Rule 20 *(e)*).

Case 5. A cuts the ball just over the net, and it returns to A's side. B, unable to reach the ball, throws his racket and hits the ball. Both racket and ball fall over the net on A's Court. A returns the ball outside of B's Court. Does B win or lose the point?

Decision. B loses the point (Rule 20 *(e)* and *(h)*).

Case 6. A player standing outside the service Court is struck by a service ball before it has touched the ground. Does he win or lose the point?

Decision. The player struck loses the point (Rule 20 *(g)*), except as provided under Rule 14 *(a)*.

Case 7. A player standing outside the Court volleys the ball or catches it in his hand and claims the point because the ball was certainly going out of court.

Decision. In no circumstances can he claim the point:

(1) If he catches the ball he loses the point under Rule 20 *(g)*.

(2) If he volleys it and makes a bad return he loses the point under Rule 20 *(c)*.

(3) If he volleys it and makes a good return, the rally continues.

RULE 21

Player Hinders Opponent

If a player commits any act which hinders his opponent in making a stroke, then, if this is deliberate, he shall lose the point or if involuntary, the point shall be replayed.

USTA Comment: *'Deliberate' means a player did what he intended to do, although the resulting effect on his opponent might or might not have been what he intended. Example: a player, after his return is in the air, gives advice to his partner in such a loud voice that his opponent is hindered. 'Involuntary' means a non-intentional act such as a hat blowing off or a scream resulting from a sudden wasp sting.*

Case 1. Is a player liable to a penalty if in making a stroke he touches his opponent?

Decision. No, unless the Umpire deems it necessary to take action under Rule 21.

Case 2. When a ball bounds back over the net, the player concerned may reach over the net in order to play the ball. What is the ruling if the player is hindered from doing this by his opponent?

138

Decision. In accordance with Rule 21, the Umpire may either award the point to the player hindered, or order the point to be replayed. (See also Rule 25).

Case 3. Does an involuntary double hit constitute an act which hinders an opponent within Rule 21?

Decision. No.

USTA Comment: *Upon appeal by a competitor that an opponent's action in discarding a "second ball" after a rally has started constitutes a distraction (hindrance), the Umpire, if he deems the claim valid, shall require the opponent to make some other and satisfactory disposition of the ball. Failure to comply with this instruction may result in loss of point(s) or disqualification.*

RULE 22

Ball Falls on Line

A ball falling on a line is regarded as falling in the Court bounded by that line.

USTA Comment: *In matches played without officials, it is customary for each player to make the calls on all balls hit to his side of the net, and if a player cannot call a ball out with surety he should regard it as good. See The Code.*

RULE 23

Ball Touches Permanent Fixture

If the ball in play touches a permanent fixture (other than the net, posts, singles sticks, cord or metal cable, strap or band) after it has hit the ground, the player who struck it wins the point; if before it hits the ground, his opponent wins the point.

Case 1. A return hits the Umpire or his chair or stand. The player claims that the ball was going into Court.

Decision. He loses the point.

USTA Comment: *A ball in play that after passing the net strikes a pipe support running across the court at the base of the net is regarded the same as a ball landing on clear ground. See also Rule 20(e).*

RULE 24

A Good Return

It is a good return:

(a) If the ball touches the net, posts, singles sticks, cord or metal cable, strap or band, provided that it passes over any of them and hits the ground within the Court; or

(b) If the ball, served or returned, hits the ground within the proper Court and rebounds or is blown back over the net, and the player whose turn it is to strike reaches over the net and plays the ball, provided that neither he nor any part of his clothes or racket touches the net, posts, singles sticks, cord or metal cable, strap or band or the ground within his opponent's Court, and that the stroke is otherwise good; or

(c) If the ball is returned outside the posts, or singles sticks, either above or below the level of the top of the net, even though it touches the posts or singles sticks, provided that it hits the ground within the proper Court; or

(d) If a player's racket passes over the net after he has returned the ball, provided the ball passes the net before being played and is properly returned; or

(e) If a player succeeds in returning the ball, served or in play, which strikes a ball lying in the Court.

USTA Comment: *i.e., on his court when the point started; if the ball in play strikes a ball, rolling or stationary on the court, that has come from elsewhere after the point started, a let should be called. See USTA Comment under Rule 20g.*

Note to Rule 24: In a singles match, if, for the sake of convenience, a doubles Court is equipped with singles sticks for the purpose of a singles game, then the doubles posts and those portions of the net, cord or metal cable and the band outside such singles sticks shall at all times be permanent fixtures, and are not regarded as posts or parts of the net of a singles game.

A return that passes under the net cord between the singles stick and adjacent doubles post without touching either net cord, net or doubles post and falls within the area of play, is a good return. **USTA Comment:** *But in doubles this would be a "through" — loss of point.*

Case 1. A ball going out of Court hits a net post or singles stick and falls within the lines of the opponent's Court. Is the stroke good?
Decision. If a service: no, under Rule 10 *(c)*. If other than a service: yes, under Rule 24 *(a)*.
Case 2. Is it a good return if a player returns the ball holding his racket in both hands?
Decision. Yes.
Case 3. The service, or ball in play, strikes a ball lying in the Court. Is the point won or lost thereby? **USTA Comment:** *A ball that is touching a boundary line is considered to be "lying in the court".*
Decision. No. Play must continue. If it is not clear to the Umpire that the right ball is returned a let should be called.
Case 4. May a player use more than one racket at any time during play?
Decision. No; the whole implication of the Rules is singular.
Case 5. May a player request that a ball or balls lying in his opponent's Court be removed?
Decision. Yes, but not while a ball is in play. **USTA Comment:** *The request must be honored.*

RULE 25

Hindrance of a Player

In case a player is hindered in making a stroke by anything not within his control, except a permanent fixture of the Court, or except as provided for in Rule 21, a let shall be called.

Case 1. A spectator gets into the way of a player, who fails to return the ball. May the player then claim a let?
Decision. Yes, if in the Umpire's opinion he was obstructed by circumstances beyond his control, but not if due to permanent fixtures of the Court or the arrangements of the ground.
Case 2. A player is interfered with as in Case No. 1, and the Umpire calls a let. The Server had previously served a fault. Has he the right to two services?
Decision. Yes: as the ball is in play, the point, not merely the stroke, must be replayed as the Rule provides.

Case 3. May a player claim a let under Rule 25 because he thought his opponent was being hindered, and consequently did not expect the ball to be returned?

Decision. No.

Case 4. Is a stroke good when a ball in play hits another ball in the air?

Decision. A let should be called unless the other ball is in the air by the act of one of the players, in which case the Umpire will decide under Rule 21.

Case 5. If an Umpire or other judge erroneously calls "fault" or "out", and then corrects himself, which of the calls shall prevail?

Decision. A let must be called unless, in the opinion of the Umpire, neither player is hindered in his game, in which case the corrected call shall prevail.

Case 6. If the first ball served — a fault — rebounds, interfering with the Receiver at the time of the second service, may the Receiver claim a let?

Decision. Yes. But if he had an opportunity to remove the ball from the Court and negligently failed to do so, he may not claim a let.

Case 7. Is it a good stroke if the ball touches a stationary or moving object on the Court?

Decision. It is a good stroke unless the stationary object came into Court after the ball was put into play in which case a let must be called. If the ball in play strikes an object moving along or above the surface of the Court a let must be called.

Case 8. What is the ruling if the first service is a fault, the second service correct, and it becomes necessary to call a let either under the provision of Rule 25 or if the Umpire is unable to decide the point?

Decision. The fault shall be annulled and the whole point replayed.

USTA Comment: *See Rule 13 and Explanation thereto.*

RULE 26

Score in a Game

If a player wins his first point, the score is called 15 for that player; on winning his second point, the score is called 30 for that player; on winning his third point, the score is called 40 for that player, and the fourth point won by a player is scored game for that player except as below:

If both players have won three points, the score is called deuce; and the next point won by a player is scored advantage for that player. If the same player wins the next point, he wins the game; if the other player wins the next point the score is again called deuce; and so on, until a player wins the two points immediately following the score at deuce, when the game is scored for that player.

USTA Comment: *In matches played without an umpire the Server should announce, in a voice audible to his opponent and spectators, the set score at the beginning of each game, and (audible at least to his opponent) point scores as the game goes on. Misunderstandings will be avoided if this practice is followed.*

RULE 27

Score in a Set

(a) A player (or players) who first wins six games wins a set; except that he must win by a margin of two games over his opponent and where necessary a set is extended until this margin is achieved.

(b) The tie-break system of scoring may be adopted as an alternative to the advantage set system in paragraph (a) of this Rule provided the decision is announced in advance of the match.

USTA Comment: *See the Tie-Break System in the appendix of this book.*

In this case, the following Rules shall be effective:

The tie-break shall operate when the score reaches six games all in any set except in the third or fifth set of a three set or five set match respectively when an ordinary advantage set shall be played, unless otherwise decided and announced in advance of the match.

The following system shall be used in a tie-break game.

Singles

(i) A player who first wins seven points shall win the game and the set provided he leads by a margin of two points. If the score reaches six points-all the game shall be extended until this margin has been achieved. Numerical scoring shall be used throughout the tie-break game.

(ii) The player whose turn it is to serve shall be the server for the first point. His opponent shall be the server for the second and third points and thereafter each player shall serve alternately for two consecutive points until the winner of the game and set has been decided.

(iii) From the first point, each service shall be delivered alternately from the right and left courts, beginning from the right court. If service from a wrong half of the court occurs and is undetected, all play resulting from such wrong service or services shall stand, but the inaccuracy of station shall be corrected immediately it is discovered.

(iv) Players shall change ends after every six points and at the conclusion of the tie-break game.

(v) The tie-break game shall count as one game for the ball change, except that, if the balls are due to be changed at the beginning of the tie-break, the change shall be delayed until the second game of the following set.

Doubles

In doubles the procedure for singles shall apply. The player whose turn it is to serve shall be the server for the first point. Thereafter each player shall serve in rotation for two points, in the same order as previously in that set, until the winners of the game and set have been decided.

Rotation of Service

The player (or pair in the case of doubles) who served first in the tie-break game shall receive service in the first game of the following set.

Case 1. At six all the tie-break is played, although it has been decided and announced in advance of the match that an advantage set will be played. Are the points already played counted?

Decision. If the error is discovered before the ball is put in play for the second point, the first point shall count but the error shall be corrected immediately. If the error is discovered after the ball is put in play for the second point the game shall continue as a tie-break game.

Case 2. At six all, an advantage game is played, although it has been decided and announced in advance of the match that a tie-break will be played. Are the points already played counted?

Decision. If the error is discovered before the ball is put in play for the second point, the first point shall be counted but the error shall be corrected immediately. If the error is discovered after the ball is put in play for the second point an advantage set shall be played.

142

Case 3. If during the tie-break in a doubles game a partner receives out of turn, or a player serves out of rotation, shall the order of receiving, or serving as the case may be, remain as altered until the end of the game?
Decision. Yes.

RULE 28
Maximum Number of Sets
The maximum number of sets in a match shall be 5, or, where women take part, 3.

RULE 29
Role of Court Officials
In matches where an Umpire is appointed, his decision shall be final; but where a Referee is appointed, an appeal shall lie to him from the decision of an Umpire on a question of law, and in all such cases the decision of the Referee shall be final.

In matches where assistants to the Umpire are appointed (Linesmen, Net-cord Judges, Foot-fault Judges) their decisions shall be final on questions of fact except that if in the opinion of an Umpire a clear mistake has been made he shall have the right to change the decision of an assistant or order a let to be played. When such an assistant is unable to give a decision he shall indicate this immediately to the Umpire who shall give a decision. When an Umpire is unable to give a decision on a question of fact he shall order a let to be played.

In Davis Cup matches or other team competitions where a Referee is on Court, any decision can be changed by the Referee, who may also instruct an Umpire to order a let to be played.

The Referee, in his discretion, may at any time postpone a match on account of darkness or the condition of the ground or the weather. In any case of postponement the previous score and previous occupancy of Courts shall hold good, unless the Referee and the players unanimously agree otherwise.

Case 1. The Umpire orders a let, but a player claims that the point should not be replayed. May the Referee be requested to give a decision?
Decision. Yes. A question of tennis law, that is an issue relating to the application of specific facts, shall first be determined by the Umpire. However, if the Umpire is uncertain or if a player appeals from his determination, then the Referee shall be requested to give a decision, and his decision is final.

Case 2. A ball is called out, but a player claims that the ball was good. May the Referee give a ruling?
Decision. No. This is a question of fact, that is an issue relating to what actually occurred during a specific incident, and the decision of the on-court officials is therefore final.

Case 3. May an Umpire overrule a Linesman at the end of a rally if, in his opinion, a clear mistake has been made during the course of a rally?
Decision. No, unless in his opinion the opponent was hindered. Otherwise an Umpire may only overrule a Linesman if he does so immediately after the mistake has been made.

USTA Comment: *See Rule 17, Case 1.*

Case 4. A Linesman calls a ball out. The Umpire was unable to see clearly, although he thought the ball was in. May he overrule the Linesman?

Decision. No. An Umpire may only overrule if he considers that a call was incorrect beyond all reasonable doubt. He may only overrule a ball determined good by a Linesman if he has been able to see a space between the ball and the line; and he may only overrule a ball determined out, or a fault, by a Linesman if he has seen the ball hit the line, or fall inside the line.

Case 5. May a Linesman change his call after the Umpire has given the score?

Decision. No. If a Linesman realizes he has made an error, he must call "correction" immediately so that the Umpire and players are aware of his error before the score is given.

Case 6. A player claims his return shot was good after a Linesman called "out". May the Umpire overrule the Linesman?

Decision. No. An Umpire may never overrule as a result of a protest or an appeal by a player.

RULE 30
Continuous Play and Rest Periods

Play shall be continuous from the first service till the match be concluded.

(a) Notwithstanding the above, after the third set, or when women take part the second set, either player is entitled to a rest, which shall not exceed 10 minutes, or in countries situated between Latitude 15 degrees North and Latitude 15 degrees South, 45 minutes and furthermore, when necessitated by circumstances not within the control of the players, the Umpire may suspend play for such a period as he may consider necessary.

If play is suspended and is not resumed until a later day the rest may be taken only after the third set (or when women take part the second set) of play on such later day, completion of an unfinished set being counted as one set.

If play is suspended and is not resumed until 10 minutes have elapsed in the same day the rest may be taken only after three consecutive sets have been played without interruption (or when women take part two sets), completion of an unfinished set being counted as one set.

Any nation and/or committee organizing a tournament, match or competition, other than the International Tennis Championships (Davis Cup and Federation Cup), is at liberty to modify this provision or omit it from its regulations provided this is announced before play commences.

USTA Rules Regarding Rest Periods

Regular MEN's and WOMEN's, and MEN's and WOMEN's Amateur — Paragraph (a) of Rule 30 applies, except that a tournament using tie-breaks may eliminate rest periods provided advance notice is given.

BOYS' 18 — All matches in this division shall be best of three sets with NO REST PERIOD, except that in interscholastic, state, sectional and national championships the FINAL ROUND may be best-of-five sets. If such a final requires more than three sets to decide it, a rest of 10 minutes after the third set is mandatory. Special Note: In severe temperature-humidity conditions the Referee may rule that a 10-minute rest may be taken in a Boys' 18 best-of-three before the third set. However, to be valid this must be done before the match is started, and as a matter of the Referee's independent judgment.

BOYS' 16, 14 and 12, and GIRLS' 18, 16, 14 and 12 — All matches in these categories shall be best of three sets. A 10-minute rest before the third set is MANDATORY in Girls' 12, 14 and 16, and BOYS' 12 and 14. The rest period is OPTIONAL in GIRLS' 18 and BOYS' 16. (Optional means at the option of any competitor).

All SENIOR divisions (35 and over), Mother-Daughter, Father-Son and similar combinations: Under conventional scoring, all matches best of three sets, with rest period at any player's option.

When 'NO-AD' scoring is used in a tournament the committee may stipulate that there will be no rest periods. Two conditions of this stipulation are: (1) Advance notice must be given on entry blanks for the event, and (2) The Referee is empowered to reinstate the normal rest periods for matches played under unusually severe temperature-humidity conditions; to be valid, such reinstatement must be announced before a given match or series of matches is started, and be a matter of the Referee's independent judgment.

USTA Comment: *When a player competes in an event designated as for players of a bracket whose rules as to intermissions and length of match are geared to a different physical status, the player cannot ask for allowances based on his or her age, or her sex. For example, a female competing in an intercollegiate (men's) varsity team match would not be entitled to claim a rest period in a best-of-three-sets match unless that were the condition under which the team competition was normally held.*

(b) Play shall never be suspended, delayed or interfered with for the purpose of enabling a player to recover his strength or his breath.

(c) A maximum of 30 seconds shall elapse from the moment the ball goes out of play at the end of one point to the time the ball is struck for the next point. In the event such first serve is a fault, then the second serve must be struck by the Server without delay.

The Receiver must play to the reasonable pace of the Server and must be ready to receive when the Server is ready to serve within the permitted time.

When changing ends a maximum of one minute thirty seconds shall elapse from the moment the ball goes out of play at the end of the game to the time the ball is struck for the first point of the next game.

The Umpire shall use his discretion when there is interference which makes it impossible for the server to serve within that time.

These provisions shall be strictly construed. The Umpire shall be the sole judge of any suspension, delay or interference, and after giving due warning he may disqualify the offender.

Note: A Tournament Committee has discretion to decide the time allowed for a warm-up period prior to a match. It is recommended that this does not exceed five minutes.

Case 1. A player's clothing, footwear, or equipment (excluding racket) becomes out of adjustment in such a way that it is impossible or undesirable for him to play on. May play be suspended while the maladjustment is rectified?

Decision. If this occurs in circumstances outside the control of the player, a suspension may be allowed. The Umpire shall be the sole judge of whether a suspension is justified and the period of the suspension.

Case 2. If, owing to an accident, a player is unable to continue immediately, is there any limit to the time during which play may be suspended?

Decision. No allowance may be made for natural loss of physical condition. In the case of accidental injury the Umpire may allow a one-time, three minute suspension for that injury. Play must resume in three minutes. However, the organizers of international circuits and team events recognized by the ITF may extend this if treatment is necessary.

USTA Comment: *Case 2 refers to an important distinction that should be made between a disability caused by an accident during the match, and disability attributable to fatigue, illness or exertion (examples: cramps, muscle pull, vertigo, strained back). Accidental loss embodies a sprained ankle or actual injury from such mishaps as collision with netpost or net, a cut from a fall, contact with chair or backstop, or being hit with a ball, racket or other object. An injured player shall not be permitted to leave the playing area. If, in the opinion of the Umpire, there is a genuine toilet emergency, a bona fide toilet visit by a player is permissible and is not to be considered natural loss of condition.*

Case 3. During a doubles game, may one of the partners leave the Court while the ball is in play?

Decision. Yes, so long as the Umpire is satisfied that play is continuous within the meaning of the Rules, and that there is no conflict with Rules 35 and 36.

USTA Comment: *When a match is resumed following an interruption exceeding 10 minutes necessitated by weather or other unusual conditions, it is allowable for the players to engage in a "re-warm-up," using the balls that were in play at the time of the interruption, with the time for the next ball change not being affected. The duration of the re-warm-up will be as follows: 0-10 minutes delay, no warm-up; 11-20 minutes delay, 3 minutes warm-up; more than 20 minutes delay, 5 minutes warm-up.*

RULE 31

Coaching

During the playing of a match in a team competition, a player may receive coaching from a captain who is sitting on the court only when he changes ends at the end of a game, but not when he changes ends during a tie-break game.

A player may not receive coaching during the playing of any other match.

The provisions of this rule must be strictly construed. After due warning an offending player may be disqualified.

Case 1. Should a warning be given, or the player be disqualified, if the coaching is given by signals in an unobtrusive manner?

Decision. The Umpire must take action as soon as he becomes aware that coaching is being given verbally or by signals. If the Umpire is unaware that coaching is being given, a player may draw his attention to the fact that advice is being given.

Case 2. Can a player receive coaching during the ten minute rest in a five set match, or when play is interrupted and he leaves the court?

Decision. Yes. In these circumstances, when the player is not on the court, there is no restriction on coaching.

Note: The word "coaching" includes any advice or instruction.

RULE 32

Changing Balls

In cases where balls are changed after an agreed number of games, if the balls are not changed in the correct sequence the mistake shall be corrected when the player, or pair in the case of doubles, who should have served with new balls is next due to serve.

The Doubles Game

RULE 33

The above Rules shall apply to the Doubles Game except as below.

RULE 34

The Doubles Court

For the Doubles Game, the Court shall be 36 feet (10.97m.) in width, i.e. 4½ feet (1.37m.) wider on each side than the Court for the Singles Game, and those portions of the singles side-lines which lie between the two service-lines shall be called the service side-lines. In other respects, the Court shall be similar to that described in Rule 1, but the portions of the singles side-lines between the base-line and service-line on each side of the net may be omitted if desired.

USTA Case 1. In doubles the Server claims the right to stand at the corner of the court as marked by the doubles sideline. Is the foregoing correct or is it necessary that the Server stand within the limits of the center mark and the singles sideline?

Decision. The Server has the right to stand anywhere back of the baseline between the center mark extension and the doubles sideline extension.

RULE 35

Order of Service in Doubles

The order of serving shall be decided at the beginning of each set as follows:

The pair who have to serve in the first game of each set shall decide which partner shall do so and the opposing pair shall decide similarly for the second game. The partner of the player who served in the first game shall serve in the third; the partner of the player who served in the second game shall serve in the fourth, and so on in the same order in all the subsequent games of a set.

Case 1. In doubles, one player does not appear in time to play, and his partner claims to be allowed to play single-handed against the opposing players. May he do so?
Decision. No.

RULE 36

Order of Receiving in Doubles

The order of receiving the service shall be decided at the beginning of each set as follows:

The pair who have to receive the service in the first game shall decide which partner shall receive the first service, and that partner shall continue to receive the first service in every odd game throughout that set. The opposing pair shall likewise decide which partner shall receive the first service in the second game and that partner shall continue to receive the first service in every even game throughout that set. Partners shall receive the service alternately throughout each game.

Case 1. Is it allowable in doubles for the Server's partner to stand in a position that obstructs the view of the Receiver?
Decision. Yes. The Server's partner may take any position on his side of the net in or out of the Court that he wishes. **USTA Comment:** *The same is true of the Receiver's partner.*

RULE 37

Service Out of Turn in Doubles

If a partner serves out of his turn, the partner who ought to have served shall serve as soon as the mistake is discovered, but all points scored, and any faults served before such discovery, shall be reckoned. If a game shall have been completed before such discovery, the order of service remains as altered.

USTA Comment: *For an exception to Rule 37 see Case 3 under Rule 27.*

RULE 38

Error in Order of Receiving in Doubles

If during a game the order of receiving the service is changed by the Receivers it shall remain as altered until the end of the game in which the mistake is discovered, but the partners shall resume their original order of receiving in the next game of that set in which they are Receivers of the service.

RULE 39

Service Fault in Doubles

The service is a fault as provided for by Rule 10, or if the ball touches the Server's partner or anything which he wears or carries; but if the ball served touches the partner of the Receiver, or anything which he wears or carries, not being a let under Rule 14(a) before it hits the ground, the Server wins the point.

148

RULE 40
Playing the Ball in Doubles

The ball shall be struck alternately by one or other player of the opposing pairs, and if a player touches the ball in play with his racket in contravention of this Rule, his opponents win the point.

USTA Comment: *This means that, in the course of making one return, only one member of a doubles team may hit the ball. If both of them hit the ball, either simultaneously or consecutively, it is an illegal return. The partners themselves do not have to "alternate" in making returns. Mere clashing of rackets does not make a return illegal, if it is clear that only one racket touched the ball.*

If you have a rules problem, send full details, enclosing a stamped self-addressed envelope, to Nick Powel, USTA Tennis Rules Committee, 3147 South 14th Street, Arlington, Virginia, 22204, and you will be sent a prompt explanation.

APPENDIX
Regulations for Making Tests Specified In Rule 3

1. Unless otherwise specified all tests shall be made at a temperature of approximately 68° Fahrenheit (20° Centigrade) and a relative humidity of approximately 60 per cent. All balls should be removed from their container and kept at the recognized temperature and humidity for 24 hours prior to testing, and shall be at that temperature and humidity when the test is commenced.

2. Unless otherwise specified the limits are for a test conducted in an atmospheric pressure resulting in a barometric reading of approximately 30 inches (76cm.).

3. Other standards may be fixed for localities where the average temperature, humidity or average barometric pressure at which the game is being played differ materially from 68° Fahrenheit (20° Centigrade), 60 per cent and 30 inches (76cm.) respectively.

Applications for such adjusted standards may be made by any National Association to the International Tennis Federation and if approved shall be adopted for such localities.

4. In all tests for diameter a ring gauge shall be used consisting of a metal plate, preferably non-corrosive, of a uniform thickness of one-eighth of an inch (.32cm.) in which there are two circular openings 2.575 inches (6.54cm.) and 2.700 inches (6.86cm.) in diameter respectively. The inner surface of the gauge shall have a convex profile with a radius of one-sixteenth of an inch. (.16cm.). The ball shall not drop through the smaller opening by its own weight and shall drop through the larger opening by its own weight.

5. In all tests for deformation conducted under Rule 3, the machine designed by Percy Herbert Stevens and patented in Great Britain

under Patent No. 230250, together with the subsequent additions and improvements thereto, including the modifications required to take return deformations, shall be employed or such other machine which is approved by a National Association and gives equivalent readings to the Stevens machine.

6. Procedure for carrying out tests.

(a). Pre-compression. Before any ball is tested it shall be steadily compressed by approximately one inch (2.54 cm.) on each of three diameters at right angles to one another in succession; this process to be carried out three times (nine compressions in all). All tests to be completed within two hours of precompression.

(b) Bound test (as in Rule 3). Measurements are to be taken from the concrete base to the bottom of the ball.

(c) Size test (as in paragraph 4 above).

(d) Weight test (as in Rule 3).

(e) Deformation test. The ball is placed in position on the modified Stevens machine so that neither platen of the machine is in contact with the cover seam. The contact weight is applied, the pointer and the mark brought level, and the dials set to zero. The test weight equivalent to 18 lb. (8.165kg.) is placed on the beam and pressure applied by turning the wheel at a uniform speed so that five seconds elapse from the instant the beam leaves its seat until the pointer is brought level with the mark. When turning ceases the reading is recorded (forward deformation). The wheel is turned again until figure ten is reached on the scale (one inch [2.54 cm.] deformation). The wheel is then rotated in the opposite direction at a uniform speed (thus releasing pressure) until the beam pointer again coincides with the mark. After waiting ten seconds the pointer is adjusted to the mark if necessary. The reading is then recorded (return deformation). This procedure is repeated on each ball across the two diameters at right angles to the initial position and to each other.

The Tie-break System

A tournament committee must announce before the start of its tournament the details concerning its use of tie-breaks. A tournament that has been authorized by the USTA or by a USTA Section to use VASSS No-Ad scoring may use the 9-point tie-break in any set played under No-Ad; it may change to the 12-point tie-break in its later rounds. No-Ad scoring is authorized for tournaments held at the Sectional Championship level and below, and for consolation matches in any tournament (excluding any USTA National Junior Championship). Other than the foregoing exceptions, all sanctioned tournaments using tie-breaks will use only the 12-point tie-break. Rule 27 establishes the procedure for the 12-point tie-break game. For a more detailed explanation see below.

If a ball change is due on a tie-break game it will be deferred until the second game of the next set. A tie-break game counts as one game in reckoning ball changes. The score of the tie-break set will be written 7-6 (x) or 6-7 (x), with the score of the winner of the match entered first, followed by the score of the tie-break game in parentheses, such as (10-8) or (8-10), with the score of the winner of the match again entered first. Changes of ends during a tie-break game are to be made within the normal 30 seconds allowed between points.

The 12-Point Tie-Break

Singles: A, having served the first game of the set, serves the first point from the right court; B serves points 2 and 3 (left and right), A serves points 4 and 5 (left and right); B serves point 6 (left) and after they change ends, point 7 (right); A serves points 8 and 9 (left and right); B serves points 10 and 11 (left and right), and A serves point 12 (left). A player who reaches 7 points during these first 12 points wins the game and set. If the score has reached 6 points all, the players change ends and continue in the same pattern until one player establishes a margin of two points, which gives him the game and set. Note that the players change ends every six points, and that the player who serves the last point of one of these 6-point segments also serves the first point of the next one (from right court). For a following set the players change ends, and B serves the first game.

Doubles follows the same pattern, with partners preserving their serving sequence. Assume A-B versus C-D, with A having served the first game of the set. A serves the first point (right); C serves points 2 and 3 (left and right); B serves points 4 and 5 (left and right); D serves point 6 (left) and the teams change ends. D serves point 7 (right); A serves points 8 and 9 (left and right); C serves points 10 and 11 (left and right); B serves point 12 (left). A team that wins 7 points during these first 12 points wins the game and set. If the score has reached 6 points all, the teams change ends. B then serves point 13, (right) and they continue until one team establishes a two-point margin and thus wins the game and set. As in singles, they change ends for one game to start a following set, with team C-D to serve first.

The 9-Point Tie-Break

Singles: With A having served the first game of the set, he serves points 1 and 2, right court and left: then B serves points 3 and 4, right and left. Players change ends. A serves points 5 and 6, right and left, and B serves points 7 and 8, right and left. If the score reaches 4 points all B serves point 9, right or left at the election of A. The first player to win 5 points wins the game and set. The players stay for one game to start the next set, and B is the first server.

Doubles: The same format as in singles applies, with each player serving from the same end of the court in the tie-break game that he served from during the set. (Note that this operates to alter the sequence of serving by the partners on the *second*-serving team. With A-B versus C-D, if the serving sequence during the set was A-C-B-D the sequence becomes A-D-B-C in the tie-break.)

VASSS No-Ad Scoring

The No-Ad procedure is simply what the name implies: the first player to win four points wins the game, the 7th point of a game becoming a game point for each player. The receiver has the choice of advantage court or deuce court to which the service is to be delivered on the 7th point. If a No-Ad set reaches 6-games all a tie-break shall be used which is normally the 9-point tie-break.

Note: The score-calling may be either in the conventional terms or in simple numbers, i.e., "zero, one, two, three, game."

Cautionary Note

Any ITF-sponsored tournament should get special authorization from ITF before using No-Ad.

*Reprinted with the permission of the United States Tennis Association. A copy of the *Rules of Tennis and Cases and Decisions* in booklet form may be purchased for $ .50 plus $1.00 for postage and handling from the USTA Education and Research Center, 729 Alexander Road, Princeton, NJ 08540, (609) 452-2580.